T0354132

FREEDOM AT WORK
Founding Principles for Business Success

The Dream of Freedom

J.M. Murff

iUniverse, Inc.
Bloomington

Freedom at Work
Founding Principles for Business Success

Copyright © 2012 J.M. Murff

iUniverse books may be ordered through booksellers or by contacting:

iUniverse
1663 Liberty Drive
Bloomington, IN 47403
www.iuniverse.com
1-800-Authors (1-800-288-4677)

ISBN: 978-1-4759-5750-1 (sc)
ISBN: 978-1-4759-5749-5 (hc)
ISBN: 978-1-4759-5748-8 (e)

Library of Congress Control Number: 2012919923

Printed in the United States of America

iUniverse rev. date: 11/9/2012

To my children:

Dianne Michelle
David Michael
Michael Joseph
Jennifer Marguerite
Joseph Jesse
Marguerite Rebekah
Jesse Paul
Paul Scott
Scott Daniel
Daniel Jeremy
Jeremy James

ACKNOWLEDGMENTS

In bringing forth a comprehensive new body of expertise in the field of business, I obviously built upon the work of hundreds of authors and practitioners, far too many for me to mention by name. The one person I would like to mention by name is Dr. Lennis Knighton, former director of Brigham Young University's Romney Institute of Public Management who launched me on my quest to redefine organizational science.

Contents

Preface

Throughout history, mankind has been driven by a dream, and that dream is *the dream of freedom*. This dream has elicited mankind's most noble attributes and has led to the development of humankind's highest potential for achieving happiness and fulfillment. America's founding fathers could not have more accurately crystallized mankind's deepest desire than they did when they identified that dream as the quest for "life, liberty, and the pursuit of happiness." When mankind has failed in this quest, that failure has invariably been accompanied by the departure from the universal model for the development of human potential, that of *developmentship* (the concept of using work to develop and liberate people rather than using people to get work done), a concept authored by our Creator and embedded in America's founding documents.

The United States of America has come closer to implementing the "developmentship" model and actualizing the dream of freedom and the pursuit of happiness for its citizens than any other nation in history. But now that dream, the American Dream, is becoming more and more difficult for the common person to achieve. Good-paying American jobs are being exported at an ever-increasing rate. More and more of our children are being lost to drugs, broken families, and moral depravity, all of which make the American Dream increasingly elusive for emerging generations. As I watch my eight sons and three daughters work their ways through college and enter the workplace, I have a deep self-interest in seeking to bring forth solutions for this profoundly disturbing trend.

In more than thirty years of intensive research in behavioral science and organizational performance, I have identified seven new paradigms for tapping the vast reservoir of latent potential in American workers. These new foundations are essential if the United States is to restore its leadership in job creation and bring our jobs back home. It is my dream to see the United States restore its global leadership in providing abundant jobs that are productive enough to justify compensation that can still deliver the American Dream. And in my career-long quest, I believe I have discovered the wellspring of American innovativeness and new job creation in this universal model of developmentship.

The paradox of the Developmentship Model is the concept that work exists to build people rather than people existing to get work done. The person is the product; profit, growth, stock price, earnings, market share, and return on investment are the measures of success for the enterprise. It is the model that must replace the old *management* paradigm if America is to bring its jobs back home and create the vast number of new jobs needed to provide meaningful and well-paying careers for the host of new knowledge workers who are graduating from America's universities.

I became aware of the need to revolutionize knowledge-worker performance when, after several years as a field engineer, I moved into the office as a manager. I found no clear definition of knowledge-work processes, little useful, real-time feedback on performance, and a dearth of team brainstorming sessions. I observed highly talented people either micromanaged or virtually free to do anything they felt like, seldom or never participating in meetings with their teammates to brainstorm work-process improvements. My perception appeared to be confirmed by an extensive review of Peter Drucker's works in the early 1980s in which he identified making the knowledge worker productive as business leadership's greatest challenge for the emerging global economy.

In this review, I was also surprised that while acknowledging that we did not yet have an integrated and holistic model of business, and that while we needed new business theory, Drucker, our greatest business authority, admitted that he did not have a new theory to offer. I was again disappointed when Peters and Waterman's's incredibly well-researched *In Search of Excellence*—while offering its highly useful *eight attributes of business excellence*—failed to offer new paradigms for business leadership, or an integrated theory of business, also indicating that, hopefully, we were still moving toward one.

Having discovered and proven the validity of the developmentship paradigm in my own worldwide experience as a leader of workers of all kinds, I conducted an exhaustive search of business literature during subsequent years, seeking to fully define and document this paradigm.

During this research, I sought the elusive, integrated theory of business that Peter Drucker and most other authorities indicated we were moving toward. Not finding it, I set out to derive the first integrated and comprehensive theory of business. I worked with models and metaphors all the way from galaxies down to the atom. Finally, I settled upon a sailing ship within our world of enterprise, the global economy, as my metaphor. It is a special kind of ship, a *Development Ship*.

For the first time, with this metaphor, a business can be viewed and understood with all of its internal dynamics (also known as disciplines) and external contingencies. Not surprisingly, this ship's destination is the dream of freedom for its passengers and crew. It sails upon oceans of opportunities, seas of competition, environments of concern, and realms of adversity. It is propelled by the winds of change and the dynamics of developmentship (seven crucial business disciplines for developing human potential and stakeholder value). Finally, it has its anchors of survival.

Also, during this period, a new model emerged for analyzing business performance called Derived Solutions Logic (DSL) or more simply, the Developmentship Model. This model is like a telescope and a microscope; it makes possible a comprehensive and holistic analysis of business from the inside out and the outside in. It is a way for the leadership and the people to collaborate online to address in a balanced way, for the first time, the developmental needs of their business and to continuously improve their organization and job performance.

Along the way, I sought to solve the problem of real-time feedback on performance for the knowledge worker. Having spent twenty-five years in a process industry, I knew that annual feedback on performance could never serve to improve knowledge-worker performance. Since all work is a process, and since no process can be in control without real-time feedback, I knew that somehow a method had to be developed to provide knowledge workers with near real-time feedback on their performance. That solution and a valid way of replacing the annual performance appraisal are also presented.

Organization structure also appeared to me to be in serious need of a new metaphor. The timeworn and overly simplistic pyramid is not adequate for the complexity of today's world of enterprise. I settled upon our solar system as the ideal metaphor for organization structure. Its spherical structure is representative of the structure of the universe—from the galaxy down to the atom.

The organization is held together by gravitational influence—the mission, vision, values, and real-time feedback on performance hold the various parts of an organization in their proper orbits. This influence is in the center, not at the top or bottom. All parts of the system are in full view of the center of the system; with today's networking technology, its interactivity is unhampered by pyramidal layers. I believe it is the right metaphor for the twenty-first-century business. Some problems that exist in sustaining teamwork in America where individualism still reigns supreme are addressed, and some solutions are suggested.

Finally, at the heart of America's job crisis are the currently flawed and fragmented business curricula and MBA programs. This book addresses this challenge with a new way to teach business, the *derivational approach,* with holistic metaphors and models.

Introduction

This book is designed to be a primer in business theory, a handbook for navigating the global economy, and a textbook for business schools. Its premise is that the best way to maximize organizational performance is for the leadership to focus its energy primarily upon developing its people and liberating them to deliver exemplary products and services. It has been abundantly demonstrated that this practice, which I call *developmentship*, when accompanied by other sound business principles, will invariably result in the maximization of profit, growth, return on investment, and stakeholder wealth.

England sought to colonize America for profit, and in due time, we, the people, drove them out. Our founding fathers then established a government for life, liberty, and the pursuit of happiness. National economic production was seen as the by-product, not the purpose, of the nation. The quest for the dream of freedom, the American Dream, upon which the government was founded, attracted the best people from all over the world, and the motivational power of this revolutionary new system quickly led to the most prolific economy in history.

For a time after World War II, General MacArthur and Japanese business leaders saw the purpose of all Japanese organizational endeavors as rebuilding individual freedom and liberty for the Japanese people. Business leaders established the growth and development of the *people* of their organizations as the purpose of the business.

Within twenty years, Japan, even without America's favorable geography, abundant natural resources, and well-educated workforce, began to globally dominate many industries with this paradigm. By the mid-1970s, Japan was in the process of appropriating 30 percent of our auto industry, and many other of our manufacturing and high-tech industries were all but taken over. Japan's business leaders eventually reverted to the profit motive, and their economy has been stagnant almost ever since.

The need for new theory was brilliantly illuminated by Bob Waterman and Tom Peters in their now classic *In Search of Excellence.* While they neglected to mention Henri Fayol, the French mining engineer who first formally introduced (in *General and Industrial Management,* published in France, 1910) the military metaphor for modern business organizations, they did outline in some detail his classic military metaphors. These models include the pyramid structure, authoritarian leadership, unity of command, mission clarity, defined strategy, etc., and they accurately observed that these timeworn metaphors were not adequate for the modern enterprise.

They then mentioned other metaphors that have and are now being suggested by various organizational scientists. Some of these are seesaws, space stations, pizza pies, champions, and skunk works. There have been many other useful but fragmented metaphors proposed. From these examples, it is apparent that holistic and truly representative metaphors for the modern enterprise have not heretofore been identified. Addressing that void is one of the primary purposes of this work.

My conviction is that until culturally embedded, holistic metaphors for enterprise are adopted, we cannot have an integrated theory of business and the innovativeness needed to retain our jobs in the face of cheap offshore labor and to create the millions of needed new jobs. This work introduces new models, metaphors, and paradigms for redefining organizational science and business leadership. Its intent is to ennoble the purpose of enterprise, to reorient the compasses of both workers and leaders, and to challenge twenty-first-century leaders and professors to see their work as being the same as that of the founding fathers, even the work of building the dream of freedom for both individuals and societies.

I challenge both the business world and the academic community to flesh out and refine my metaphors, tools, and techniques—and to create an extensive body of empirical data on the power of the developmentship paradigm.

My mission was to lead the way to new frontiers of organizational and individual performance. It is time for the business world to develop this frontier, rise to a new threshold of innovation and competitiveness, and bring our jobs back home.

Calvin Coolidge said, "The business of America is business." And the real business of America has always been to bring the dream of freedom to life.

CHAPTER 1
The Void and the Challenge

*"Defining a new paradigm for business that honors
sustaining the planet through people, processes, and
profits is a worthy cause and a formidable challenge for
the twenty-first century economic community."*
—Darlene Collins

There is a great need for new theory in business. While there has been a modern revolution in information technology, organizational science has changed little since Henri Fayol introduced his fourteen principles of business management in 1910. Even at this late date, Fayol's principles still represent the closest thing to a comprehensive theory of business we have ever had. This reality and the lack of a modern integrated theory of business strikingly confirm the poverty of today's organizational science.

Trying to manage a business in today's highly complex global economy with current archaic organizational science is not unlike the problem that confronted the wonderful ship *Titanic* in trying to navigate the Atlantic Ocean at night. Without the extensive measures that are now employed to warn ships of impending disaster from colliding with undetected giant icebergs, the *Titanic* was doomed to failure. Similarly, the loss of millions of American jobs to offshore competitors and the disappearance of entire American industries is, to a large degree, a result of this void in today's organizational science.

In *Management,* the late Peter Drucker, our greatest business authority, said, "We do not have a genuine theory of business and no integrated discipline of business management."[1] Fifteen years later, Peters and Waterman, with all of their research and consulting, still could not derive one.[2] And until now we have never had an integrated theory of business. This void has caused us to have to teach business in a fragmented way. As a result, the MBA has come under attack from many noted business authorities, such as Edward Wrapp, Steve Lohr, Jeffrey Pfeffer,[3] and the venerable Henry Mintzberg.[4]

As already mentioned, we are still laboring at this late date with archaic paradigms in the field of business introduced more than a hundred years ago in Fayol's *General and Industrial Management.* Work by Max Weber and others eighty years ago resulted in the emergence of the now almost universally scorned annual performance appraisal. Many more of our current management paradigms are archaic and inadequate for the information economy we now live in.

Statistical Process Control was developed by the Bell Laboratories in 1939 and used in the war effort during the US industrial miracle of World War II, after which W. Edwards Deming took it to Japan and led a worldwide manufacturing revolution with it. While it is

---

1   Drucker, *Management,* (New York: Harper & Row:1980),49.
2   Peters and Waterman, *In Search of Excellence,* (New York: Harper & Row, 1982), 29–36.
3   Pfeffer and Long, *The End of Business Schools,* (The Academy of Management Journal: 2002).
4   Mintzberg, *Managers, Not MBA's,* (New York: Berrett-Koehler 2004.)

still viable and valuable in the manufacturing realm, until now, no comparable technology has been devised for the now-dominant knowledge-work processes.

There has never been a widely used, sustainable model of teamwork for the highly individualistic American worker. A few pioneering companies have succeeded in creating one, such as W. L. Gore and Associates with their lattice structure and others, but this approach has not caught on widely. Instead, American business leaders have tried to import the quality circle, which hasn't worked all that well on a sustained basis. Total Quality Management and reengineering have also been used as platforms for engendering sustained teamwork in the American business community. They, however, also appear to fade over time in sustaining teamwork in the United States. And there have been other unsuccessful approaches.

Indeed, there have been virtually no substantial innovations in organizational science for a hundred years with the possible exception of Alfred P. Sloan's model of federalization for the large corporation. While the lattice, the matrix, the inverted pyramid, the pizza-pie organizational form, and others have been used with success by a few companies, in most companies, the pyramid structure, effectively, still reigns supreme, and its gross oversimplification of today's complex organization is indicative of the poverty of organizational science.

And in our information economy, with our highly liberated workforce, we are still wedded to the archaic concept of *management*, again with a few exceptions, such as W. L. Gore and Associates and a relatively few others.

Finally, business education is still a matter of teaching a number of independent disciplines and trying to tie them together with case studies, simulations, and the like. No current business school teaches business as an integrated whole. Without an integrated theory of business, it has been impossible to teach business holistically from the beginning so that students come to understand the importance of addressing all of the disciplines of business all of the time in a supercompetitive global economy.

I believe that this condition—which is manifesting itself in many areas of business in the form of business failures, relentless mergers, and acquisitions with their inevitable downsizing and exporting of American jobs abroad, executive greed, and loss of investor confidence—represents a great opportunity for progressive business leaders of today.

Essential to the ushering in of this new age, I believe, is the bringing forth of seven new conceptual foundations for the twenty-first-century business and business education. The first is the replacement of the archaic paradigm of management itself with an entirely new discipline of *developmentship*.

It is a needed paradigm shift from seeing people as instruments to get work done to that of seeing work as a means of developing human potential. Instead of customer service, business solutions, high-quality technology, and hardware being the products, they become the tools for building the real product: the people of the organization. The person has to be the leadership's product in the new *Age of Developmentship*.

Japan's business leaders used this philosophy in the '70s, and '80s to bring about a manufacturing revolution and take over a lot of our industries. Some American companies have approximated this philosophy and have inevitably been the leaders. Jack Welch affirmed the competitive power of fostering the growth of people, and GE has consistently been one of the leading businesses of the world in many markets.

I personally experienced the power of this philosophy in my years with GE. I can honestly say that I do not believe I would be alive today had it not been for a wonderful supervisor I had when I was totally self-destructing and underperforming in the late 1960s. Had he not put my welfare ahead of the multimillion-dollar projects I was endangering, I would not have had any hope of turning my life around.

Bill Marriott and Bill Marriott Jr. embodied this same philosophy in building and sustaining great performance from the Marriott

Corporation over the years. In fact, all of the eight attributes of excellence identified in the still highly relevant *In Search of Excellence* were essentially about people.

With this new paradigm, the former manager becomes the *Career Facilitator,* and the former team member, associate, front-line employee, etc., becomes a *strategic improviser,* derived from work by Lee Tom Perry in *Real-Time Strategy.* At the core of the organization, providing strategic direction is the leadership—not at the top or the bottom, but at the center of a spherical organization.

The next desperately needed new paradigm is an integrated theory of business. The twenty-first-century business must have entirely new, living, holistic, and culturally embedded metaphors and a new *purpose;* that purpose is to develop human potential and to help bring the dream of freedom to life. After their extensive study of excellent businesses, Tom Peters and Bob Waterman indicated that, if we are to institute change, we must have powerful and clear metaphors. But while, as mentioned earlier, many metaphors have been suggested and tried, none of them are holistic in nature.

The *Development Ship* embodies many of our deeply treasured "ships," such as fellowship, friendship, workmanship, leadership, and entrepreneurship. And ships have consistently been the essential vehicles of the migration to the land of freedom since the Vikings and before.

This ship is driven by the winds of the innate human need to make a difference, the desire for a better quality of life, and the need for personal growth and spiritual fulfillment, which together constitute the dream of freedom that burns within each of us. As with Maslow's's hierarchy of human needs, it has a hierarchy of dynamics. What Maslow discovered was that the lower needs motivated only until they were fulfilled, but that the higher needs increased in their motivational strength as they were experienced. People development and innovation are these higher needs in organized endeavor. The more people experience these dynamics in the workplace, the more motivated and productive they become.

This Development Ship sails in a global economy upon *oceans of opportunity, seas of competition,* and *environments of concern;* it sails in *realms of adversity;* it has its *anchors of survival,* and it is propelled by the *winds of change,* and empowered by the *dynamics of developmentship,* otherwise known as the disciplines of business, all of which are dynamics for developing human potential and helping to bring the dream of freedom to life for its people.

With these holistic metaphors, we can finally derive an integrated theory of business, graphically portray all of the facets of a global economy together, and begin to understand and teach business as an integrated whole. This model is the *Seven Determinants of Global Competitiveness* that I describe in chapter 6.

In today's economy, structure no longer follows strategy as Alfred Chandler postulated. In *Offensive Strategy,* Lee Tom Perry said, "Strategy is structure and structure is strategy." It is essential, therefore, that we identify a comprehensible and understandable metaphor of organization structure that can convey all of the interactiveness, dynamism, and ever-changing nature of the twenty-first-century business. And that metaphor is the spherical structure.

The universe is structured spherically from galaxies down to atoms. This metaphor places the leadership in the center with teams of people revolving around the leadership; the organization is held together by the gravitational pull of mission, vision, values, a superordinate goal, supporting strategic objectives, and performance-maximizing organizational metrics. A few organizations and authors have approximated this structure, but the metaphor remains to be fully developed, which I now challenge business leaders to do.

With the new model of the global business and our Development Ship, there needs to be a powerful new navigation system for this ship. That navigation system must be based on real-time feedback. The DSL (Derived Solutions Logic, or simply the Developmentship Model), along with real-time feedback on the knowledge-work processes is both a method of strategic direction-finding and a way to enable strategic improvising at every orbit and within every team of the organization.

Executives can use the model to chart the organization's strategic direction by constantly strengthening, clarifying, and communicating the leadership dynamic I call the *dream of freedom* and assuring that their people are continuously deriving the essentials of the other six dynamics. At the same time, the seven determinants are addressed holographically by the organization. They are constantly treated derivationally and collaboratively by the leadership and by the work teams in each of the other disciplines.

This kind of continuous organization development can now be easily carried out via LANs (local area networks), enterprise-wide networks, and the Internet. People can now sit at their computers and engage in derivative, team-based activity that will elicit their best and most creative performance. This kind of structure provides, because of its real-time and computer-based nature, when supplemented with occasional face-to-meetings, a model of teamwork for the highly individualistic American worker that can finally be sustained on an ongoing basis.

Using the DSL model and the new integrated theory of business, the leadership and people would identify derivationally and holistically, for the first time, all of the essentials of the oceans of opportunity, those of the seas of competition, and so forth, comprising the organization's external contingencies. The same would apply to the organization's internal dynamics or disciplines, those of innovation, production (the discipline of quality), finance, and so forth. This holistic approach metaphorically replaces dead reckoning navigation of a business in a complex global economy with a more accurate and modern global positioning system.

The leadership would begin to spend most of its time addressing the Seven Determinants of Global Competitiveness (the external contingencies of the business) and the strategic internal dynamic of the *dream of freedom* (mission, vision, values, metrics, etc.), while the people would continually address the other dynamics of the business. This kind of work would finally add the holism and balance to navigating a business in a global economy that has long been missing and that has often resulted in the loss of market share to offshore competition.

Central to the Development Ship's navigational system is real-time feedback on work-process performance such as that used by Deming and others to lead a worldwide revolution in manufacturing quality and productivity. Benjamin Franklin used this same real-time feedback process to become, arguably, history's most productive mortal. And this new paradigm, I believe, is essential to a needed revolution in knowledge-work performance. Since all work is a process, and since no process can be highly productive without real-time feedback, it follows that, without this new paradigm, the knowledge-work environment will continue to grossly underperform.

The currently dominant paradigm in the American knowledge-work environment is still the highly dysfunctional annual performance appraisal, which Deming called, "the worst thing US management does" (as indicated to an audience at the Utah State University's Partners Program in 1991, at which I was in attendance). Having had many of them during my forty-year career, I can personally testify of their counter-productiveness. One of my last ones, during which I had what I thought was one of my most successful years, I was hammered because the leadership was pursuing a strategy and goals other than the ones we had agreed upon a year earlier. They thought I was off course and had not said a word about it for the whole year. I felt like one of those calves in a rodeo that running full speed, is suddenly roped, jerked around by the neck, and then thrown down and tied up.

We need to move to a new system that combines the best of inertial, celestial, and cybernetic guidance principles, a way to, for the first time, actually quantify and chart the knowledge-worker processes and ultimately quantify individuals' and teams' contributions to the bottom line of the corporation. This process is fully defined and quantified in appendix II.

The next paradigm I believe American business leadership will have to adopt is a new paradigm for business leadership itself. Our current crisis in business is abundant evidence of this need. There must be a *Chrysalis Leadership Experience*, a metamorphosis in business leadership, from the current paradigm of plying the waters of mergers and acquisitions to that of pollinating the existing organization's people.

Finally, America's business schools must move to an entirely new and more highly effective way of teaching business principles to augment the current case study, contingency, simulations, and other methods in use. This method, I believe, is the *derivational* method, using DSL and other derivational models and the integrated theory of business to derive the essentials of global competitiveness that are unique to each organization.

I am proposing a new conceptual foundation for the twenty-first-century business and for business education. The developmentship paradigm is in harmony with the highest achievers in business. When leaders put people's growth and development first, give them ennobling strategic direction, and deliver real-time feedback, they invariably go out and deliver profits, legendary customer service, consistent innovation, and global leadership.

This was Jan Carlzon's philosophy and the paradigm he used to turn Scandinavian Airlines around in a single year after fifteen years of losses to years of consistent profits and high customer esteem. This was the philosophy that that Sam Walton used to build the world's largest, most dynamic, and globally competitive corporation. In *Made in America,* he explained that he focused on his people's growth and development first, and they went out and conquered the world for him. This work, the work of developing human potential, of letting the person be the product and the monetary and other measures the natural by-products of this process, is the most powerful of leadership paradigms.

It is the same paradigm that the incomparable John Wooden used to win ten national championships in his last twelve years as basketball coach at UCLA, with four undefeated seasons, a feat never achieved before or since. He never spoke to his team of winning games or championships. He focused totally upon building character and eliciting from each player his best every time and all the time. The system he developed was designed to empower each player to achieve his full potential—athletically and morally—with winning as the natural by-product of this process. The player was the product and not the tool he used to win championships.

The real power of this paradigm, I believe, lurks in Einstein's formula for the energy that can be released from an enriched uranium atom. If you empower people with a clear mission, an inspiring vision, ennobling values, real-time feedback, subject them head-to-head to world-class competition, and share the gains with them, a nuclear explosion of globally competitive performance can be generated without the harmful radiation. There will be fallout to be sure, but it is inevitably in the form of positive effects and influences on the business environment and in the lives of people.

What is the rationalization of these normative concepts in view of the academicians' demand for statistical substantiation and empirical data to support theoretical foundations? What more substantiation should be needed than to look at the phenomenal growth of our nation's economy, a nation founded on the developmentship paradigm? When compared to the Soviet Union's experiment with a centrally planned, command-and-control economy, the disparity in the cumulative gross national products of the United States versus the old Soviet Union over seventy years of communism is astounding. And when applied in Japan after World War II, to an economy and its industrial base literally in ashes, the developmentship paradigm produced a globally competitive Japan in a mere twenty years.

Developmentship is the most powerful of all paradigms for maximizing labor utility and business profitability. It embodies the most deeply held values, norms, and ideals of people. It can be quantitatively validated, as demonstrated with the new business economics (see chapter 8). Businesses that have aligned their values closely with the societies in which they operate have invariably released the maximum amount of human energy and have maximized their global competitiveness and profitability even in negative business cycles.

Again, the developmentship paradigm has been abundantly substantiated by the financial performance of both economies and corporations that have utilized it. It can be argued that even the Great Depression was precipitated by the reductive behavior of business leaders during the twenties and early thirties. And the climb of our country out of the Depression was led by the great Franklin D. Roosevelt. Just prior to his election to his first term, he said, "These unhappy times call for the building of plans that put their faith once more in the forgotten man at the bottom of the economic pyramid."[5]

Ronald Reagan used this same philosophy to inspire and empower American business to produce a GNP during the 1980s that could support both guns and butter and eventually brought down the Soviet Union and ended the cold war.

As John Kennedy would no doubt have expressed the challenge to American business leaders, "Ask not what your people can do for you, but ask what you can do for your people." So I am challenging American business leadership to usher in a new age of business, to reinvent business enterprise for the twenty-first century, and to do as the great pioneering leaders of all ages have done: *bring the dream of freedom to life.* Only by replacing the current paradigms of excessive personal enrichment, paper entrepreneurship, incessant downsizing and exporting of jobs, and shortsighted accounting, with this higher ideal, and by using new tools to apply to the enterprise the very old principles upon which free societies are founded, can the business leader maximize the performance of the twenty-first-

---

5   Manchester, William, *The Glory and the Dream,*(New York: Random House, 2008), 46.

century organization. This strategy of *using work to build people, communities, and societies* is the best of all strategies for maximizing earnings and achieving globally competitive leadership.

On June 12, 1987 President Ronald Reagan, speaking at the Brandenburg Gate in Berlin said, "Mr. Gorbachev, tear down this wall." If he were president today, I believe he would put it this way to American business leadership: "American executives, bring America's jobs back home."

I am confident that—as the East Germans did tear that wall down (with the help of people from all over the world)—American executives will tear down old, archaic business paradigms that hold back the American worker and will bring our jobs back home.

CHAPTER 2
The Age of Developmentship

*The concept that work exists to develop and liberate people
(developmentship), rather than that people exist to get work
done (management), is the great performance paradox
and the ultimate performance-maximizing principle.*

The American economy has experienced six successive ages or eras
since its beginning: the *agricultural era,* the *craftsmanship era,* the
manufacturing era, the *service era,* the *high-technology era,* and the
current *information economy,* the age of the Internet. During the
twenty-first century, the economy must move fully into a seventh
era—the *era of people development and innovation,* which I call
the *developmentship era.* This age is that in which organizational
balance, innovation, and the development of human potential become
paramount if we are to create sufficient numbers of quality jobs for
our people.

Each prior age of the economy has been a natural and necessary
stage in the development of the greatest economy in the history of
mankind. Each era dominates until technology and culture mature
to the degree that the new stage emerges to become paramount.
The crowning age in this evolutionary process is the long-awaited

period in which the individual will truly become more important than profits, growth, net worth, and all of the other factors (all essential by-products of developmentship) that have so long subverted the development of human potential.

It is not that the development of the individual has not been important in business. It has even been paramount in some of the great companies, such as Southwest Airlines. Indeed, some of the premier Japanese companies used this powerful philosophy to build companies that quickly destroyed entire American industries and took 30 percent of the American automobile market during the 1970s and 1980s.

After the publishing of *In Search of Excellence* in the early 1980s, American companies rushed to a customer-driven philosophy, almost universally declaring that the customer was number one. True, the customer must be number one with a maximizing organization's front line people. But, for the leadership, the most energizing and empowering philosophy is that of putting the growth and development of his or her people first, the concept of of *Developmentship*. Companies that have used this approach to business have almost invariably been the leaders in their fields of endeavor. When people sense that they are the organization's primary product and that the work of legendary customer service is the organization's strategy for developing their full career potential, they become tremendously motivated and highly innovative in delivering quality products and superior customer service.

The Age of Developmentship is, in reality, the coming of full circle in the stages of human development in America. The age of the small farm in early America was the embodiment of almost all of the elements of human development. Autonomy, universal public education, the free market, teamwork (in the form of total family involvement), real-time feedback on performance (the observable daily results of hard work), the need for invention and constant innovation, the fostering of the country's founding values, and all of the other aspects engendering and empowering personal growth were present.

While the lack of communications, transportation, and other modern conveniences necessarily limited human development, the development of the most important of all human qualities—*integrity* and *character*—could not have found a richer environment in which to have been engendered than that of the small farm. It is not surprising that the American farm industry is still the most efficient of American industries and remains unsurpassed in the world for its productiveness.

Following the agricultural era, came the age of craftsmanship, not replacing the age of agriculture, but building upon it. The age of craftsmanship was essential because the economy was lacking an industrial base to fill the need for products with which to build a new nation and satisfy the human needs of pioneers and immigrants in the new country. *Craftsmanship* called forth the uniqueness, the special skills and talents, and the development of people's ability to deliver service and quality. But craftsmanship, while yielding high-quality products, could not deliver the volume required for a rapidly growing populace in the new nation of America. Technological breakthroughs in the late 1800s and early 1900s ushered in the *age of manufacturing*.

The age of manufacturing made possible for the first time in any country a truly dominant middle class. And after World War II, the world could not get enough American products for the next twenty years. But Japan and a number of third-world countries learned how to manufacture quality products with great efficiency; by the mid-1970s, manufacturing in the United States was on the decline. By the end of the 1970s, the country was moving toward a service economy. The age of technology and the age of the service economy developed almost simultaneously, one fueling the other. Almost everything became computerized, and service quality in many sectors was revolutionized.

Then came the Internet. By the late 1980s, a new way of doing business and accessing and exchanging information had burst upon the scene. And by the mid-1990s, the information age was in full swing. By the turn of the century, the inevitable shakeout of the dot-coms was in progress. But the nature of enterprise had been forever changed. With incredible communications and distribution networks, everyone having a computer, and the Generation X workforce firmly entrenched, the American economy was finally ready for the Age of Developmentship.

The Age of Developmentship will require an entirely new discipline to replace the old practice of management. It will require new paradigms of organization structure, new ways to teach business principles, new measures of white-collar performance, a new metaphor for enterprise, and at long last, an integrated theory of business.

The Need for New Theory

"We do not have a genuine theory of business and no integrated discipline of business management."
Peter Drucker, *Management, Tasks, Responsibilities, Practices*, p. 49

"Certainly, we are not proposing a complete theory of organizing here. But that is not to say that there is no need for new theory. The need is desperate if today's managers, their advisors, and the teachers of tomorrow's managers in the business schools are to be up to the challenges we posed in Chapter 2."
Peters and Waterman, *In Search of Excellence*, p. 102

"We have created a monster. The business schools have done more to insure the success of the Japanese and West German invasion of America than any one thing I can think of."
—H. Edward Wrapp

"There is now a widely held view that the MBA might be part of the current problem."
—Steve Lohr, *The New York Times*

Seven Needed New Paradigms for the Twenty-First-Century Business

- an enlightened new discipline to replace the archaic concept of "management"
- an integrated theory of business and new business economics
- a new global navigation system for business
- a new metaphor for organization structure
- real-time feedback for the knowledge-work environment
- a new paradigm of business leadership
- a new way to teach business principles

CHAPTER 3
The New Discipline

The Career Facilitator must replace the manager in the
workplace, inasmuch as the person's development is the
product of the organization, with legendary customer service
and high-quality products the tools for this development,
and great financial results, the natural by-product.

Before we can define the new discipline that is to replace management, we must finally come to know what the product of the knowledge worker is. Alas, we now know that it is the person doing the work, the knowledge worker himself or herself. The end products are not invoices, customer satisfaction, engineering solutions, or service, but in all cases, they are the growth and development of the organization's people. The primary business of all organizations is the building of people and helping bring their dreams of freedom to life. The new paradigm is that the person does not exist to get the work done, but that the work exists to build the person. The person is the product.

We can identify the career-development process and establish standards of excellence for it. The process can be measured by the associate himself or herself. The individual can measure this process on a real-time basis. The process can be constantly corrected and improved. And it is this personal growth that constitutes the most deeply held value of the knowledge worker. The knowledge worker thinks, *I must be constantly growing. I must be enhancing my value and preparing myself to make my maximum contribution to an ever-changing work environment.* The realization that the person is the product in the work environment is the *performance paradox.* It is the paradox that has escaped us for so long that we have understandably assumed that, with the myriad outputs in the office environment, any attempt to quantify and measure knowledge-worker productivity and processes would be futile. The current paradigm is that customer satisfaction is the goal, and we spend all of our efforts surveying our customers. But the person is the product, and customer satisfaction is the desired outcome, the natural by-product of teams of highly productive knowledge workers in the new economy. While we must survey the customer, the right way to improve customer satisfaction is to improve our products and our service-delivery processes by tapping the enormous creative capacity of our people and to periodically *reinvent* our industries.

The reason that the person is the right product is simply that the very purpose of this society is to promote life, liberty, and the pursuit of happiness for the individual. By making the person the product, the organization is placing itself in perfect harmony with this purpose, the development of the individual's potential for a productive, happy life. Such an organizational value system for the first time fully merges the organization's goals with those of its associates and lays the foundation for unleashing the enormous untapped potential of the knowledge worker.

The other half of the new paradigm is that *service quality* is the right process for making the knowledge worker highly productive. We can define and measure this process on a real-time basis as well. We know that, with the definition of these two processes, *career development* and *service quality,* we can finally provide process measures, establish standards of excellence for these processes and, for the first time, empower the knowledge worker to become highly productive and fully achieving of his or her potential.

With this new realization, we must move away from the current paradigm that people are just one of many assets, or *resources*, even if viewed as the organization's most valuable resource, and that the personnel function in organizations is the *human resources department*. It is time to move to the new concept of human beings as the central participants in a lifetime, career-development, and service-delivery process. They are the *product* of the organization. It is time to overhaul the human resources department and rename it the *Career-Development Department,* or simply the *People Department* (as Southwest Airlines calls it), with the mission of helping maximize the potential of every one of the organization's individuals. Nothing is more motivational than this focus on people's growth and development.

The Needed Paradigm Shift

de-vel-op-ment-ship \de-'vel-ep-ment-ship\ n.
[Fr. *developper*] a. the skill of eliciting creative
potential from people b. the process of using work
as a tool to develop people and maximize
organizational performance

man-age-ment \'man-ij-ment\ n. [root Fr. L. *man-us,* hand] a. the act of handling, controlling, or
directing b. the use of a means to accomplish
an end

With this understanding, we can define the new discipline. It is *Career Facilitator.* No longer is the job to handle and control workers, but it is to counsel with people for the purpose of developing the full career potential of the person. It is to define, measure, and bring about continuous improvement in the career-development and service-quality processes.

Another critical and major part of the job is to help secure, for the organization's people, opportunities for gainsharing and the ability to earn a wage proportional to their contribution to the bottom line. This new work is called *developmentship*.

The products of this new discipline are highly productive and fully achieving people. No longer are the principal concerns profits, customer satisfaction, hardware, or software, but people. The new Career Facilitator must arrive at the office each day with a clear perception of what business he or she is in. No longer is the job getting the work out. It is now the building of people. Upon perceiving this new attitude and being provided with the tools of self-control, the people will get the work out as never before—with great enthusiasm and in great quantity. It is still right and proper to manage things, namely one's time, one's workspace, or one's own career quest. But one must cease forever to assume that people can be managed for high performance.

The new processes are *career development* and *service quality*. Maximizing the performance of these processes is a great deal more motivational than monitoring the pursuit of goals because processes are real-time and require real-time (immediate and continuous) measurement and feedback. Goals, by their discrete nature, are achieved more infrequently and do not generate the constant feedback that processes do. As always, it is essential to set and achieve goals, although the goals should be established on a monthly or quarterly basis rather than on an annual basis in today's fast-moving environment. But just as important, is the generation of real-time feedback on performance.

The necessary credentials for the new work of developmentship are a passion for developing human potential, a deep understanding of human motivation, and a great ability to listen to people with a genuine interest in their hopes, dreams, and career aspirations. The Career Facilitator must understand that people are motivated by a deep concern for their quality of life, their growth, and their desire to give their special gift, to make their unique contribution, and to actualize their full potential.

The new skill required is the skill of facilitation, the ability to elicit innovation and draw out people's creative ideas (even from the introvert), to be patient, and to seek consensus. Achieving consensus, which is analyzing an issue long enough and with the proper tools so that the right solution eventually emerges, is time consuming and requires a yielding of power, from the former boss to the new team. But it is the right way to solve most problems in the workplace and to achieve the greatest commitment to the implementation of the solution.

Finally, the tools of developmentship are the new approaches to structured synergy, such as online collaboration (see appendeces V&VI) and real-time feedback on performance, along with *food, fun, and facts*. They are the pizza parties, the celebrations of excellence, the expressions of appreciation, and the sharing of information, including the disclosure of appropriate financial data to every member of the organization. And perhaps the most important facts are the process measures generated by the people themselves, the individual performance graphs on their computers and posted outside their workspaces, and for the team, in a common area. Because ultimately, if these graphs are not generated and posted, the work processes will, with certainty, be out of control and far less than fully productive.

This, then, is the job description and definition of the new discipline. With it, let us give the old paradigm of management a proper burial as with all relics that have lived out their time. No longer are we in management. We are now in people development. Let us begin to use the right language. It is going to take a very long time to turn around this *management* battleship and convert it into a *developmentship* carrier, a launching platform for people's full development. So let us begin.

The Implications

What are the implications of the end of management and the advent of developmentship in the workplace? Who would not like to see the almost universally despised annual appraisal die a natural death? Did not the Eastern Europeans finally cast off communism after a seventy-year trial, having experienced its devastating effects on people's productivity and performance? Yet, the West continues to hang on to the annual appraisal (arguably, equally as fundamentally flawed) long after it has been demonstrated to be detrimental to service quality and documented to be destructive of knowledge-worker productivity.

Perhaps we have hung on to the annual appraisal so long simply because we could identify no alternative to it, and we felt as if we had to do *something,* even if it was wrong. But with the new paradigms and process measures, why not just discard it? If we must have a basis for awarding annual or quarterly bonuses or annual merit increases, let us award them to the individuals who achieved both their quarterly goals and consistent levels of excellence in both process categories during the year. In deciding whom to promote, let us promote on the same basis that of not only goal achievement, but also of documented excellence in the career-development and service-quality processes.

What are the implications for the human resources departments? Its activities must expand from those of dreaming up and administering benefit packages and trying to teach people how to make the annual appraisal work (an impossible task). It must begin to include finding gainsharing opportunities for people, teaching Career Facilitators how to foster career development, and how to administer real-time feedback systems for the people.

The new *Career-Development Specialists* will begin to provide regular career counseling. They will assure that a wide array of professional and business journals are available to all of the organization's people. They will establish extensive business and professional libraries, reading rooms, and multimedia resources. And they will get into the business of teaching the art of developmentship, mentoring, and Career Facilitatorship.

What are the implications for the former manager, the new Career Facilitator? He or she will finally have a constructive basis upon which to regularly interact with his or her people. No longer will the goal be control people or to *get* the work out because the work will flow like never before. Freed from worry about production and cost, more time can be spent doing his or her own research and career development. But most of all, the new Career Facilitator will be able to experience the joy of developing human potential, working with the team, and experiencing the power of synergy.

What are the implications of the new paradigms for American businesses? The greatest hindrance to American job creation has been the massive waste of human potential in the office workplace. The wholesale elimination and exportation to low-wage offshore companies of these jobs as a result has caused real fear in the office workplace, as well as having already placed far too many of these people in the unemployment category. But this exportation of American knowledge-worker jobs and excessive downsizing is creating a massive backlash among both workers and customers in the United States.

What are needed are not fewer knowledge workers, but more productive, more innovative, and more achieving office and knowledge workers. These new paradigms, once implemented, will revolutionize the performance of people in the office, and even in the manufacturing sector, as the country unites in restoring American jobs, as it did in producing the industrial miracle of World War II.

The worldwide quality revolution, based upon Statistical Process Control (SPC) technology developed at Bell Laboratories in 1939, was initiated by the United States during the war effort of the 1940s. Having abandoned the technology following the war, in favor of the maximization of speed and volume in an effort to meet postwar, worldwide demand for American products, the technology was introduced to a desperate and hungry Japan by Deming, Juran, and others. Japan then used the technology to lead this worldwide quality revolution. Every manufacturing person had a process control chart and measured his or her own product quality. When product quality fell off due to no discernible fault of the worker, everyone stopped working, met as teams, and solved the process problems.

Deming found that quality problems were the fault of the work process more than 90 percent of the time. And he determined that output per person was far more dependent upon the *quality of the process* than the speed of the worker. That is why he redefined productivity, not as output per man-hour, but as the minimization of variation in the production process. He came to know that productivity equals process quality, not individual speed in turning out widgets.

So must the coming revolution in office productivity be driven by real-time process measurement and ever-improving process quality. The office is ripe for a revolution in productivity and innovation. If the leadership will abandon the old paradigms and adopt the new, there is the potential to see productivity improvements in the office of 100 percent or more. And if the leadership will share the gains with the people, there could be a return to American world leadership in wages and job security in the office. Freed from the fear of the annual appraisal and the fear of layoffs, enthusiasm can return to the office workplace. It can be fun to come to work again!

Why did we lose most of our small farms and millions of manufacturing jobs in spite of revolutionized farm productivity and dramatically improved blue-collar productivity? Will a revolution in the office reverse the loss of these jobs? Already we have exported millions of our knowledge-work jobs. We are also failing to create new jobs because of extraordinary productivity improvements that are being experienced from high technology and downsizing and because of a major and lingering business recession brought on by a massive debt crisis. Is there still enough untapped potential in our knowledge workforce to counter these influences?

The decline of the small farm and manufacturing in the United States resulted not from automation or dramatic increases in productivity—or because of low-cost foreign labor—but from the catastrophic waste of American human capital in the farm, the office, and manufacturing. Self-serving executives with archaic paradigms and a paternalistic Congress destroyed the soul of the small farm with subsidization instead of synergy.

The lack of innovation and cost control in manufacturing resulting from obscenely compensated, rock star executives and unions that weighed down corporations with unsustainable legacy costs allowed the Pacific Rim and third-world countries to take our manufacturing jobs.

And instead of our government being a catalyst for small farmers to reinvent the small farm with incentives to diversify and innovate, it paid farmers not to produce traditional crops that were creating unmanageable surpluses and falling prices. Had the government been an agent of collaborative synergy in the farm industry, the small farm could have been reinvented, and would have brought forth myriad new and innovative products rather than continuing to try to compete with traditional products more efficiently produced by the gigantic mega-farms.

And had manufacturing executives seen themselves in the business of building people instead of empires, the union demands would have been mitigated—and the innovations needed to keep our manufacturing base would have been forthcoming.

If dysfunctional boards of directors continue to pay their CEOs millions of dollars a year and providing golden parachutes while these CEOs are laying off thousands of their workers and paying remaining workers infinitely less than they are making, we will destroy the soul of the knowledge worker, too. We will continue to lose our information technology and knowledge-worker jobs to the third world as we did our manufacturing jobs.

Unless American business leaders begin to abandon self-aggrandizing, myopic paper entrepreneurship, get into the developmentship business, and unleash the full potential of their own workers to create new technologies and industries, American jobs will continue to disappear. Otherwise, third-world countries will invariably master the ability to duplicate our quality, productivity, and innovation in the manufacturing and high-tech areas and take our jobs.

Two examples of the kind of enlightened leadership I am proposing are Herb Kelleher of Southwest Airlines and Jim Sinegal, CEO of Costco. Kelleher has built a small, regional carrier into a leading national airline by putting his people first and the customer second, with profits a by-product of having fun at work. Sinegal limits his salary to no more than twice that of his store managers, his profit margins to 10 percent, mines the innovative potential of and pays his associates well, and continually reinvents his business. Not even mighty Wal-Mart's Sam's Club can compete with Costco and Sinegal's exemplary business ethics and selfless leadership.

And how many millionaires has Microsoft created by eliciting the full potential of its knowledge workers and continually recreating its company and its industry? Microsoft has continued to grow and dominate in its field and added knowledge workers—even in negative business cycles and in a business as tough as software development. While Microsoft's ethics have been questioned and even tried in court, it has nonetheless shown that releasing the innovative potential of people can largely obviate the need for downsizing. The same has been demonstrated by SAS, Google, Edward Jones, Wegmans Food Markets, W. L. Gore, and a number of other great companies.

So, having lost millions of our small farms and much of our manufacturing base with reductive management and poor policies, let us now move to *developmental leadership* and save our knowledge-worker jobs.

CHAPTER 4
The New Metaphors

"If I were to give off-the-cuff advice to anyone trying to institute change, I would say, 'How clear is the metaphor? How is that understood? How much energy are you devoting to it?'"
—Tom Peters

Just as the paradigms for management must be replaced, it is essential that the grossly oversimplified and dysfunctional metaphors for business now be replaced by appropriate and powerful new models. If we are to succeed in moving from getting work done through people, the concept of *management*, to using service to build people, the work of *developmentship,* we must move away from mechanistic and woefully inadequate models of business to models that embody the noblest aspirations of our people and embrace the complexity and simplicity of organizational endeavor.

One of the new metaphors is the Development Ship. Its destination is a dream, the dream of freedom of its occupants. Its purpose is to bring the dreams of its crew and passengers to life. It is on the same voyage as were the *Nina,* the *Pinta,* the *Santa Maria,* the *Mayflower,* Magellan's craft, the sampans of the South Vietnamese, the rowboats of the Cubans, and all of the boats of those who have sought to find their dream of freedom.

A Holistic Metaphor for Business

But what can be done with organization structure? The pyramid will no longer suffice. There must be a metaphor for organization structure worthy of the twenty-first century, the century of *developmentship*. This metaphor is our own solar system, encircled by diverse planets, held together by the gravitational pull of the sun, planets subsisting on the sun's energy, but independent in their own spheres.

As is our solar system, the business organization's parts are controlled by a the gravitational pull of mission, vision, and values, and are energized by the leadership's example of walking the talk of this corporate constitution, by the provision of investment capital, and by the motivational power of clear performance standards and real-time feedback on performance. The solar system has the wholeness, balance, and interactiveness to serve as the new metaphor for organization structure.

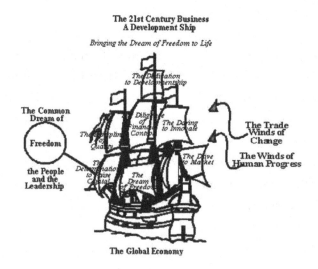

A Holistic Metaphor for Business

Now that we have identified a metaphor possessed of the essential degree of wholeness, we are ready to identify the determinants of global competitiveness. To do this, we need to apply the new model for analyzing business organizations—the *Developmentship Model.* Finally, with new metaphors and models, we can construct the long-anticipated, integrated theory of business.

Only by adopting this new theory of business (see chapter 6) can we rise to the twenty-first-century paradigm of developing human potential rather than merely enhancing shareholder wealth, finally realizing that while wealth-building is essential and is the engine of progress, it has never been the purpose of enterprise

Life is to be lived to experience the joy of freedom and personal growth. People exist to bring quality to their own lives and to the lives of others. And business organizations are essential to the actualization of this possibility.

So, let us move to the new business metaphors as we discard the concept of *management* and adopt the new paradigm of *developmentship.*

Structure Must Be Dynamic and Interactive—Much Like an Atom, a Cell, a Solar System, a Molecule

"Structure will become a dynamic enabler of both change and unchange, the ultimate model of 'organized chaos.'"
—Igor Ansoff, *In Search of Excellence,* p. 111

"Strategy is structure and structure is strategy in the case of Capitalists."
—Lee Tom Perry, *Offensive Strategy,* p. 128

The dynamic lattice structure originated by Bill Gore, portrayed three-dimensionally, becomes an interactive sphere, the right metaphor for the twenty-first-century organization.

Organization Structure for the Twenty-First-Century Business

It has long been known that the pyramid is not an adequate metaphor for organization structure. It is inherently dysfunctional for human organizations. First of all, it invariably shields the leadership from most of the organization, especially from the fertile fields of imagination deep within the traditional pyramidal structure. With this isolation from the organization's rich beds of potential innovation, it is not surprising that executives are beguiled by the more evident and tempting possibilities of mergers and acquisitions. Secondly, it tends to isolate the organization's subunits from each other, regardless of how much we try to connect them. And finally, it typically has not included customers, suppliers, and other organizational constituencies that are fundamental to the survival of the organization. While some have inverted the pyramid and begun to show customers at the top and the leadership at the bottom, the metaphor is so overly simplistic that it cannot effectively represent the globally competitive organization of the twenty-first century.

Over the years, I have tried scores of metaphors, searching for the appropriate complexity, simplicity, and wholeness with which to represent a human organization. Finally, it occurred to me that almost all of nature has a spherical structure. The universe, galaxies, solar systems, suns, planets, molecules, and atoms are all structured spherically, with controlling influences at the center and subunits rotating about them. With this realization, it became apparent that our own solar system is the ideal metaphor for the business unit and that the galaxy is the appropriate metaphor for the multinational conglomerate. While our own globe served well for the metaphor for the integrated theory of business, our solar system best represents the modern business organization.

With the leadership at the center of the organization and with today's networking technology, all parts of the organization can easily be in view of the leadership. It is essential that leaders begin to see the potential of their own organizations and spend the bulk of their time nurturing, motivating, pollinating, and developing these enormous, untapped reservoirs, rather than yielding to the temptation to continually ply the waters for possible mergers and acquisitions. While mergers and acquisitions are in some cases valid and effective ways of capturing market share and spawning innovation, they are also fraught with inherent dysfunctionalism and often thwart the innovative potential of the existing business.

Solar systems represent the diversity, complexity, beauty, balance, and wholeness that should characterize the twenty-first-century business. The analogies between these structures and the business organization are almost too numerous to mention. Suffice it to say that like businesses, they divide, merge, implode, and ultimately exist for the growth and development of humankind. So does the organization of the twenty-first century exist primarily for the development of human potential.

Changing the business structure paradigm is easily as seminal as the discovery of this continent. After Columbus made his voyages to America, redefining the structure of the world, the whole meaning of liberty and freedom eventually changed. Little did he know that he was paving the way for the greatest experiment in the unleashing of human potential in the history of mankind. Likewise, with the paradigm of spherical organization structure and the new perspective on the purpose of business—namely *developmentship*—who knows what human possibilities are beyond the present frontiers of the old pyramidal business enterprise?

The redefinition of the structure of the world from the former linear to a new understanding of the spherical nature of the earth unleashed a flood of innovation in world navigation and opened up a whole new world of opportunity for man's quest of his inherent dream of freedom. Likewise, a new understanding of the spherical nature of the organization portends completely new frontiers of development of natural and human resources.

In reality, this transformation has, to a large degree, already occurred with the transparency that has been made possible by the

Internet, local area networks, and social networks. It is contingent upon business educators and practitioners to tap the full power of this metaphor by using the new communications technologies to provide financial data and real-time feedback for all orbits of the organization.

A flood of innovation is now possible with the ability for cross-functional teams to collaborate online and for the leadership to observe and nurture this phenomenon, assuming their servant leadership roles and fueling this revolution in performance with clearly articulated missions, visions, values, and rewards commensurate with the results.

Without an appropriate model of organization, businesses are constrained to resort to the old lines of authority and reporting structures, which always imply rigidity and fail to communicate the interconnectedness and networking that must characterize today's globally competitive business. The spherical structure accurately represents the robust interactivity that must exist in the modern business organization. Following are some representations of that structure and interactivity. This metaphor is only now emerging, however, and it remains for business organizations to creatively apply it and to reinvent business organization structure.

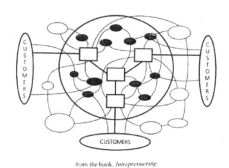

from the book, *Intrapreneuring*

Gifford Pinchott's Representation of Structure

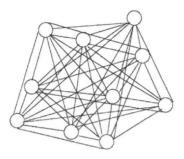

W. L. Gore's Lattice Organization Structure

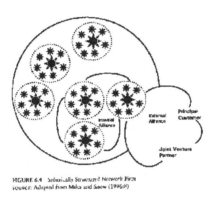

FIGURE 6.4 Spherically Structured Network Firm
SOURCE: Adapted from Miles and Snow (1996:8)

Miles and Snow Representation of Spherical Structure

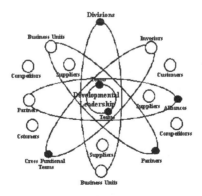

Organization Structure for the Twenty-First-Century Business
Spherical, Synergistic, Supercompetitive

The ultimate goal of the twenty-first-century business leader should be to emulate the structure of organic entities. Interestingly, all of the instructions for building the proteins of life are present in every one of the trillion or more cells of the human body. Why does the DNA code that directs all of the body's systems not reside only in, for example, the brain? Doubtless, the answer to this question is that the complexity of life requires that the information for its peak performance must be at the front line of every system, every muscle, and every organ.

Similarly, in today's supercomplex global economy, all of the information to make day-to-day decisions needs to reside as close to the front line as possible. The spherical structure can break down the walls that have so long hindered pyramidal organizations. Even with lightning-fast communications, the volume of information needed by the organization simply cannot tolerate the centralization of information.

Strategy is no longer strictly the purview of the leader. It must be real-time and front-line driven. Winning strategy is driven by real-time information. The leader's job is primarily to constantly clarify and communicate mission, vision, and values—and to provide real-time feedback.

CHAPTER 5
The Psychology of Developmentship

"Classic economic theory, based as it is on an inadequate theory of human motivation, could be revolutionized by accepting the reality of higher human needs, including the impulse to self-actualization and the love for the highest values."
—Abraham Maslow

The Hierarchy of Human Needs

The job of the skilled Career Facilitator is to bring all of the elements of process enhancement into play. Abraham Maslow, in his seminal work, *Toward a Psychology of Being,* elegantly identified the essentials of the high-achieving individual with his needs hierarchy model of human behavior. In hundreds of interviews with high-achieving individuals, he identified the principal motivators of human behavior in ascending order: the need for *safety, security, belonging, esteem,* and *self-actualization* (the progressive realization of one's special mission in life).

Maslow discovered that the motivating strength of the first four of the fundamental human needs decline as they are progressively satisfied. He found the motivational strength of the highest order need, self-actualization, increases as it is experienced. Once the individual discovers what it is that he or she is uniquely born to do, what actualizes his or her true potential, his or her personal mission in life, the doing of it is no longer work, but play, although it typically elicits the most arduous expenditure of energy on the part of the individual. That is why a peak-performance process for people must be directed toward the development of the person's full potential, or as it is related to the workplace, *career development.*

Of course, in using the career-development and customer-service process measures, both individual and team scores should be graphed and posted. And all of the innovative ways organizations typically use to recognize people, both individually and as teams, should be utilized. For example, if the team as a whole achieves a combined score of excellence in the two processes for the month, bring in pizza and celebrate. Individuals exceeding the standards for the combined process scores for the month could be given a handshake and a genuine expression of appreciation from the facilitator in his or her workspace, one-on-one, with the mention of details of noteworthy performance. Hardly anything is more satisfying to a person than for that person's facilitator to notice individual excellence in detail and to validate that person's worth and value to the organization by expressions of genuine appreciation.

But what of the other needs in this hierarchy of needs? While belonging and esteem needs are richly fulfilled by the team-centered service-quality processes and expressions of appreciation to individuals, what about the survival and security needs? These needs can only be fulfilled by adequate compensation. One approach to helping satisfy this need is the principle of *gainsharing.* This powerful principle can unleash a great deal of untapped creative potential of people in the office. Gainsharing assures that people already focused on delivering ever-improving service quality do it with the maximum cost effectiveness and introduces the motivational power of individual free enterprise into corporate life. Gainsharing, coupled with other pay-for-performance strategies made possible with the new process measures, can make peak performance in the office possible for the first time.

Today, there are approximately 2,500 companies using gainsharing, according to a study done by the American Management Association. Among the companies using the plan in their plant operations are Dresser Rand, Consolidated Diesel, Carter-Day, Dover Rotary Lift, Gradall Company, Ingersoll-Rand, Mixer Systems, Proen Products, Rexnord, Webster Electric, Cincinnati Milacron, and a host of smaller companies.

A typical result of gainsharing is General Tire's 1,950-employee plant in Mount Vernon, Illinois, which has generated $30 million in savings over a five-year period—$20 million of which was paid out to workers in the form of bonuses, while the company profited by $10 million.

People First: A Performance-Maximizing Paradigm

"A successful company puts its employees first."

[About the Company's Pathways to Independence] ...
"This sends a signal throughout the company that
this is a company that puts employees first."

"It's a matter of the climate you develop in your
company and the kind of attitude you have towards
people, that they're important, that they come first."
—J. W. Marriott Jr., Spirit to Serve

Gainsharing is a win-win approach to increasing personal incomes and reducing the cost of service. The organizational leadership says, "As a team, find ways to improve service quality and revenues while reducing waste, and we will share those gains equally with you." Of course, this approach necessitates opening the books of the organization and sharing the financial data pertaining to the team's sphere of influence.

Once people know where the money is being spent, they are extremely adept at finding waste when they know they can receive a percentage of what they save. The gainsharing process need not be overly complex. It is simply a matter of establishing what has historically been spent for operations, improvements, and capital additions, and what is planned for future improvements, and allowing people to participate in the process to improve quality, cut costs, and share in the gains.

Gainsharing often involves obtaining objective cost estimates by outside sources or the planners so that there is a valid yardstick with which to measure the effect of the team's synergy in stripping the waste from the operations or proposed projects. If these estimates are conservative and professional, the organization's leadership can feel fully justified about sharing the difference between what was actually spent and what might have been spent without the team's participation.

While gainsharing is an important facet of the art of developmentship, it has been used successfully by relatively few American companies (it is rather widely used in some European countries). Its potential has not yet nearly been realized in the American workplace. The reason for this void, I believe, is the prevailing *management* paradigm of controlling people rather than unleashing the creative potential of people and the power of synergy that the team is capable of. Nothing is more effective in eliciting teamwork and peak performance from people than gainsharing, once the career-development and customer-service process measures are in place.

The Hierarchy of Organizational Dynamics

Just as people have a hierarchy of physical and psychological needs, an organization has a hierarchy of *dynamics*. But unlike the declining motivational strength of a person's lower order psychological needs as they are fulfilled, the motivational strength of organizational dynamics builds upon and amplifies each succeeding dynamic. For example, the most fundamental dynamic, *leadership*, or the entrepreneurial dream of freedom of the founders of the enterprise fuels the dynamic of *the determination to raise capital*. Capitalization having been achieved, it becomes the driving force for the *marketing* of the product, and so forth.

Once people have a powerful sense of mission, vision, and values from the leadership, the initial sail of the Development Ship is hoisted, and the ship can get under way. Then, when the business is adequately capitalized, another sailed is raised, and the ship can begin to pick up speed. Each successive dynamic adds driving force and new energy for the achievement of the next hierarchical dynamic, the next dynamics being, highly efficient *production*, the *discipline of quality, diligent financial control*, and *the daring to innovate*. Finally, when people discover that the organization's very purpose is their own development (the crowning dynamic of *developmentship*) and are provided with conditions to unleash their full creative potential, the motivational power of this dynamic begins to multiply geometrically. When this dynamic is coupled with continuous improvement in each of the other dynamics using a tool such as Enterprise Developer (addressed in detail in chapter 14), a revolution of innovation, productivity, and quality can be unleashed.

As mentioned earlier, the power of the dynamic of *developmentship* is the very secret to the astounding economic success of America. It is a great paradox that is difficult for a business leader to grasp—even as the world has wondered at the placing of the happiness and fulfillment of the individual as the highest priority of the business of America when the founders framed the United States Constitution.

The best that legendary Peter Drucker could come up with when asked the purpose of a business was saying, "The purpose of a business is to create a customer." Conventional wisdom is that the purpose of a business is to increase shareholder wealth. In the twenty-first century, the leader who finally recognizes that his or her business is to develop the full career potential of his or her people will be the market leaders of the global economy.

The systematic introduction of these organizational dynamics to Japan's war-torn economy following World War II led this tiny nation, virtually devoid of natural resources, to General MacArthur, W. Edwards Deming, Joseph Juran, and many Japanese executives provided the founding leadership of the revolution. America provided most of the capital, and the principle market for the products. Statistical Process Control and team-driven process improvement soon led to Japan's world domination in many industries.

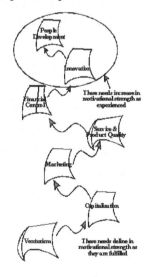

The Supercharging Effect of
People Development and Innovation

Appropriate financial controls were implemented, and tremendous innovation was fostered, out of which came an entire new body of manufacturing expertise.

Finally, many of the great Japanese executives established the growth and development of their people as their number-one priority, and they created a revolution in manufacturing quality and productivity.

American companies responded to the Japanese challenge and began to involve the front -manufacturing people in the design and improvement of the production process; manufacturing productivity and quality rose dramatically. As a result, American blue-collar workers are still the most productive in the world, and manufacturing quality now equals that of Japan. Once again, American workers have demonstrated that when they are involved in the design of the work process and in self-measuring and continually improving that process, they will out produce anyone.

With the discovery of the hierarchical nature of the seven organizational dynamics and how they relate to human physical and psychological needs, we are ready to begin constructing the long-awaited integrated theory of business and to move toward the revolution in innovation essential to the creation of millions of new jobs in the United States economy.

Developmentship and Real-Time Feedback

The work of developmentship is the work of channeling the winds of human progress, which are comprised of the collective needs, hopes, and dreams of the individuals that make up a society into the sails of the Development Ship. The leadership *and* the people build the ship, the Career Facilitators raise and set the sails, and the ship is navigated by real-time feedback on performance.

This real-time feedback process is the very same process that Columbus used to navigate the original Development Ship to the shores of America and the same process that Benjamin Franklin used to navigate his own life in becoming one of the most productive and influential people of all time.

Before the knowledge-work productivity revolution can occur, the leadership must come to realize the importance of real-time feedback on performance. Even with a genuinely valid theory of business and a well-constructed Development Ship, we will never arrive at our destination without expert navigation, using real-time feedback.

Eliciting Teamwork from American Workers

It has always been difficult to sustain quality circle type teamwork from highly individualistic American workers. Studies some years ago conducted by Rapaille International Inc., for a number of American companies have shed new light on the challenge of eliciting greater teamwork and synergy from American workers. The challenge has to do with cultural imprinting.

G. Clotaire Rapaille, cultural anthropologist and founder of Rapaille International, developed a theory that each culture has a collective, cultural *unconscious*—a pool of shared imprintings that unconsciously guide the behaviors of the members of that culture. American workers, for example, have a collective cultural subconscious or imprinting that is different from that of the Japanese mind, the French mind, and those of other cultures.

In the American worker's unconscious, teamwork must be more about one's professional development than about finding a solution. In order to sustain teamwork in America, team meetings must elicit *each* team member's *maximum* contribution to the solution. Unorganized brainstorming must be replaced with *structured synergy*. There must be the use of derivational tools, such as DSL (see chapter 11), and the orchestration of team dynamics by a skillful facilitator. Only when team members experience the personal growth that emanates from building consensus based on cutting-edge analytical tools will they be willing to tear themselves away from their cubicles and computer screens for the sustained, regular team sessions that are essential to maximizing performance in the workplace.

Teamwork in America
Differing Goals
Differing Results

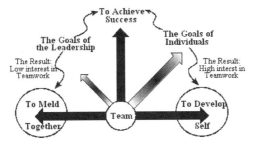

Solution: Implement team-driven gainsharing or provide career development incentives for sustained synergistic activity.
Adapted from Industry Week, May 1995

CHAPTER 6
An Integrated Theory of Business

*No business school in the country presents a business
as a whole, teaching rather a number of independent
disciplines. It is not surprising, then, that our businesses
often lurch from one fad to the next, neglecting a
balanced, holistic approach to corporate governance.*

We know that the purpose of business and the organization is to develop
human potential, build freedom, *and bring the dream of freedom to
life*. But, as Drucker said thirty-eight years ago, and as every business
writer since Drucker has said, we have never had an integrated theory
of business. With the new paradigm of *developmentship* and a new
metaphor of the business organization, it is possible to construct an
integrated theory of business and to move to new and more effective
ways of operating businesses and organizations and teaching business
principles.

Recognizing the thorough globalization of the world's economy,
we can identify the *Seven Determinants of Global Competitiveness*
for the twenty-first-century business organization. They are the
Dynamics of Developmentship (the disciplines of business), the
Environments of Concern, the *Oceans of Opportunity*, the *Seas of*

Competition, the *Realms of Adversity,* the *Winds of Change,* and the *Anchors of Survival.*

A powerful new model empowers us to derive for the first time, a comprehensive, holistic, and integrated theory of business. The *Derived Solutions Logic* utilizes Maslow's concept of hierarchical needs, the number of completeness (seven), and the literary device of alliteration to produce an elegantly simple, but incredibly powerful means of finally overcoming the inordinate complexity of modeling human organizations.

Utilizing DSL methodology, it is easy to derive, for example, the seven dynamics of developmentship, the fundamental disciplines of business. The first dynamic of developmentship is the leader's *dream of freedom,* driving the organizational ship and this same dream of those that eventually board the ship. This powerful motivational force leads to the *determination to raise capital* in order to bring the ship into existence. Then comes the *drive to market.* Next, in the hierarchy of developmental needs is the *discipline of quality,* to learn to produce products and/or service economically and of superior quality. Then is required the *diligence of financial control,* the avoidance of excessive debt-to-equity ratios and the containment of costs.

It is imperative to have the *daring to innovate* as old products become commodities with reduced margins. Finally, there must be the *dedication to developmentship,* the commitment to develop the full potential of the intellectual capital of the organization. This dedication is the motivating force that unleashes the full capabilities of the organization's people, the most important factor in remaining competitive in a supercompetitive global economy.

Having identified the dynamics of developmentship, the fundamental purpose of organizational endeavor, and the full development of the organization's people, we can easily identify the seven *essentials* of each dynamic and the seven *elements* of each essential. We can view the organization under a microscope, identify the developmental needs within each dynamic, and prioritize these needs. We can systematically improve business performance from the inside out and the outside in and achieve balance and harmony throughout the organization for the first time.

We can, for the first time, derive an integrated theory of business. Because of the extraordinary complexity of a business organization and the lack of holistic metaphors, we have never before been able to derive an integrated and comprehensive model of the large organization. Our business schools have continued to teach fragmented business disciplines, and our MBA graduates have managed fragmentally. It is time that we bring balance and wholeness to the science of business leadership.

Using our globe as the external environment, the Development Ship as the framework for the internal dynamics, and the DSL model as a derivational tool, we can now identify all seven determinants of global competitiveness.

Using the navigational tools introduced in this work and a holistic and powerful new leadership paradigm, that of *developmentship,* we can sail to new business frontiers.

The Seven Determinants of Global Competitiveness

The Seven Determinants of Global
Competitiveness

In the past, in teaching business principles, we have depended upon the fragmented nature of the contingency and case-study methods. The problem with these approaches when used alone or even together is that they have failed to lead to a holistic and integrated understanding of business principles. As a consequence, business has traditionally, and not surprisingly, lurched from fad to fad or from one pressing contingency to the next.

With this new methodology of conducting a comprehensive analysis of itself in each of the required dynamics, the organization can identify the missing essentials and elements and begin to implement the recovery strategies it needs with a great deal less reliance upon solutions from consultants. And the new theory clearly identifies the most important work of the organization's leadership—the captain and his crew. Their number-one job is keeping the dream of freedom alive and developing the full potential of their people.

The job requires a great deal of developmental thinking, and the questions they should be seeking answers to each day of their lives are: *What are our core competencies, and what services can we provide to fully develop these competencies? What are the strategic breakthroughs we need to achieve in order to develop the full potential of our people? How can we best share our financial success so that our people can earn a living wage? And, how can we use our success to build the dream of freedom?* This thinking will keep the leadership occupied for 90 percent of the time, thus freeing the people to achieve.

A Holistic Model of Business

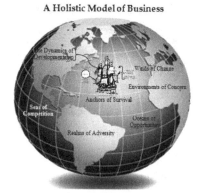

The Global Economy

CHAPTER 7
Foundational Leadership

*As an executive, ask not what your people can do
for you, but what you can do for your people.*

The Most Empowering Vision

The two greatest things a business leader can give his people are
selfless integrity and heroic vision. One man has personified these
two leadership attributes as perhaps no other mortal has. This man
was General George Washington. It is not surprising that this man's
photograph is observed hundreds of millions of times each day on the
one-dollar bill. His impact on American business simply cannot be
overestimated. Without his leadership and vision, there would not be
a United States. We would still part of the United Kingdom or of the
Commonwealth of England.

In January 1776, George Washington's bedraggled army had lost
five battles in a row against England. It was Christmas day, and the
army had been driven by German mercenaries across the Delaware
River from Trenton, New Jersey. They were exhausted, hungry, cold,
and many even without shoes. But the dream of freedom still burned
within the great father of our country, and he rallied his troops for a
surprise attack to be carried out early the following morning. Only

because of the profound respect the men had for this great general did they wrap their feet in burlap and secretly and silently cross the frozen river to attack the Hessians who were caught completely by surprise.

Washington's army decimated the Hessians and won its first great battle of the revolution. But it was eight long years before the revolution was finally won at the Battle of Yorktown. Between those years was the horrible winter at Valley Forge where 2,500 of our revolutionaries froze or starved to death and hardships by those who fought for our freedom that can never be fully appreciated. George Washington had forsaken a comfortable life on his estate in Virginia and even helped finance the war when Congress refused to at times to even provide money for uniforms and weapons.

What were the secrets of George Washington's leadership? First of all, his paradigm was not self-aggrandizement but rather selfless service. Unlike many corporate leaders of today, he was in the business of building the dream of freedom. He was born into wealth but gave it up to serve his country. He was propelled by the dream of freedom for his countrymen. Secondly, his personal integrity was so complete that he was almost worshipped by his troops and peers. The depth of his character and the clarity of his vision inspired men to fight on under the most adverse circumstances—and when there appeared to be no hope. It was his burning dream of freedom and the hand of Providence, which he constantly entreated, that finally led the revolutionary army to victory at Yorktown.

What can today's business leaders learn from George Washington? George Washington believed that every American should be on the same mission he was—to build the dream of freedom—and that every individual should find a way to advance this cause in his or her life's work. Chief executives must begin to realize that they are in the same business as the founding fathers of our country—to build the dream of freedom for their people and for their society. Rather than spend their time building empires through mergers and acquisitions, which take a tremendous amount of their time, they should refocus their attention on building the dreams of freedom of their own people by unleashing their full career potential.

Today's business leaders could also take a lesson from Washington's example of great personal sacrifice for the cause of freedom. Washington left the comfort and affluence of Mount Vernon and served without pay for eight years, eventually being reimbursed only for his personal expenses during the war. While I am not advocating that executives serve without pay, I am deploring the obscene compensation plans that seem to be a prerequisite for so many of today's CEOs.

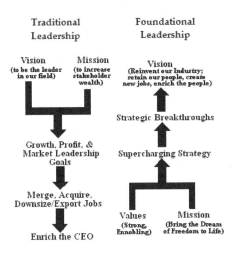

In *The Fifth Discipline*, Peter Senge relates how that it was not until five critical technologies came together in the famed DC-3, that commercial aviation was finally able, after thirty years of experimentation, to become economically viable. These technologies were the variable-pitch propeller, the retractable landing gear, lightweight metal construction, the radial, air-cooled engine, and the wing flaps. Of course, these technologies were accompanied by a redefining of the paradigms about aviation from flight as a fascinating curiosity, restricted to adventurous, barnstorming pilots, to aviation as a major form of transportation for people in general and a valuable tool for business and government service.

Similarly, the revolution in manufacturing productivity required Deming's redefinition of productivity as process quality rather than individual speed and the coming together of robotics, cellular manufacturing, just-in-time inventories, Statistical Process Control, and the empowerment of the front-line people to own, regulate, and continuously improve the manufacturing processes.

With the new integrated theory of business, the Developmentship Model, the redefinition of the paradigms and processes of knowledge-worker productivity, the new economics (see chapter 8), and the maturing of the information economy, all the essentials are in place for a revolution in business performance, a leap of progress in human productivity, and a new era of liberty and freedom.

What is the implementation process? It is essential to realize that it is not the goal to get leaner (by constant downsizing and restructuring); rather, it is essential that the organization consistently create entirely new businesses, revenues, profits, and jobs for its existing workforce. The mission must be to redefine, reinvent, and recreate the industry—and to change the paradigms that have governed the organization's field of endeavor. It must be *sea changing,* unleashing the innovative potential of its workforce to create new *businesses,* such as cellular phones, e-commerce, DVD technology, and so forth. The vision must be a shared and heroic, a singular, stretching, superordinate goal for the organization. The values must be focused—as Google's are—on people. *We want to work with great people. Technology innovation is our life's blood. Working at Google is fun.*

But there must be more than mission, vision, and values. The dream of freedom at the heart of every person requires a *strategy* that will *supercharge* the organization. And that strategy is the leadership's commitment to unleashing the full creative and productive potential of the organization's people. There must be a structure for synergy at all orbits of the organization that will allow each person to contribute his or her creative potential to the organization's success.

The leader must adopt a new paradigm of leadership, one that moves away from plying the waters of mergers and acquisitions, from consuming other organizations in search of innovation, to that of pollinating his or her own people. This transformation will require nothing less than a metamorphosis, a chrysalis experience in the leadership paradigm (see chapter 7). But this metamorphosis can occur quickly, once a leader experiences, even to a small degree, the power of developmentship. Walter Wriston, long-time CEO of Citibank, said, "The person who figures out how to harness the genius of his or her own people will blow away the competition."

There must be a spherical structure that finally breaks down the communication barriers that have characterized and often paralyzed the pyramidal organization of the past. All of the technology is now in place for the breaking down of these barriers and for the free flow of communications from the outside in and the inside out of the organization.

Then there must be scintillating symbolism that inspires the organization's people and communicates the true meaning of the organization to the customers and stakeholders of the enterprise. That symbolism includes a lofty business definition (the slogan), a logo that captivates, and lyrics that inspire (both the slogan put to music and a company song).

And finally, there must be supporting, soft and hard organizational metrics and strategic objectives focused on innovative, new solutions. These metrics must lead from the mission, vision, values, and strategy. They must be learned by every member of the organization. And they must be linked to the organizational reward system.

Thinking through the organization's core competencies—and carefully identifying what it is that it does best—will determine what kind of new paradigms and new businesses the organization should seek to create. *In terms of our customers' values, what business are we in, what business should we be in, what businesses should we abandon, and what new businesses should we create?*

With the seven essentials of the dream of freedom in place and the new Developmentship Model, we can begin to unleash the full potential of the organization. Each week, work teams collaborate online and meet for an hour to identify the dynamics, the essentials, and the elements of their aspect of the business. With this new tool, the organization can rise to the level of peak performance and achieve the balance necessary to keep the Development Ship on course to the destination of competitive leadership and the dream of freedom for each of its members.

It is apparent, with millions of American jobs having been exported to developing and third-world countries, that new plateaus of performance must be achieved by American workers if this loss of our jobs is to be reversed. America has proven that it can, when its way of life is threatened, as it was during World War II, create an industrial miracle.

With China holding a trillion dollars of our debt and unemployment at a seemingly intractable 8 or 9 percent, it is imperative for America to rise up once again and lead the way to new frontiers of innovation, productivity, and job creation. This miracle is entirely possible because of the power of the dream of freedom that wrought the astounding turnaround of America's economy from the Depression and led the way to victory over the Axis powers.

America's noble women took over many of the manufacturing jobs vacated by our soldiers, a quality and productivity revolution was driven by the Statistical Process Control technology created at the Bell Laboratories in the late 1930s, and every American sacrificed for the preservation of their dream of freedom. Hundreds of new technologies were brought forth, new industries were created out of whole cloth, and old industries transformed themselves into mighty instruments of the stuff that wars are made of.

And we can do it again with our backs to the wall and the powerful new paradigms of developmentship.

Not surprisingly, it has now become apparent that Einstein's's simple formal, $E=mC^2$, is just as valid for human energy as it is for nuclear energy. For people, the energy, $E,$ to restore America's jobs is equal to the *mass* of America's untapped human m, times, C^2, real-time feedback on the customer-service and career-development processes.

To fully release the organization's productive and innovative potential, we must unleash the power of freedom at work. What is the control system that permits the release of the full potential of an organization's people for the first time? Without real-time feedback, it has never been possible to allow people to synergize and to innovate to their full capacity. Like a nuclear reactor without control rods, people heretofore have had to be kept in narrow job definitions, unable to contribute their many untapped talents for useful innovation. Otherwise, the organization goes out of control and generates too many unmarketable products and ideas. With a real-time control system, a structure for synergy (the DSL model), and gainsharing opportunities, waste can constantly be eliminated and a floodgate of new businesses and new jobs can emerge.

As I indicated earlier, passionately putting the customer first is a powerful philosophy that many companies have used to achieve leadership in their markets. One has only to look at how Wal-Mart has fueled its ever-increasing size at the expense of low-paid employees and the loss of thousands of small-town businesses to see the problems with this strategy. Obsessiveness with low prices has also led—despite its one-time commitment to buying American—to its caving to offshore low-price suppliers and abandoning its former American suppliers. In one case, a former supplier next door to one of its new stores had to close its doors as Wal-Mart forsook it for cheaper foreign suppliers. Many of the previously well-paid employees of this one-time supplier ended up working at Wal-Mart for a fraction of their former wages. With saving its customers money and growth as its highest priorities, instead of the welfare of its own people, it has become predatorily competitive—and its employees are not making a living wage.

Had Wal-Mart's leadership stuck with Sam Walton's initial philosophy of putting its own people first, it would undoubtedly have steadily increased its profit sharing with them (begun in 1971), placing their welfare ahead of maximizing growth and market share. Instead, it has ended the profit-sharing program, replacing it with a 6 percent contribution to their retirement plans, resulting in a decrease in take-home pay. While increasing employee compensation would doubtless throttle Walmat's growth somewhat, doing so would mitigate to some degree the growing resistance of its intrusion into ever expanding market segments.

Costco has demonstrated that you can have good wages and low prices. Its experience has demonstrated that when employees liberally share profits, they not only can earn a living wage, but they also become much more loyal, innovative, and customer-focused than those working merely for a survival wage. With its better wages, Costco outperforms Wal-Mart's Sam's Club in every financial category, year after year.

Sharing a significant portion of its profits with its people in the form of quarterly bonuses (in addition to the retirement and stock purchase contributions) and releasing its innovative potential with the developmentship paradigm and concepts put forth in this work would magnify Wal-Mart's unquestionably valuable contribution of saving its customers money. It would also demonstrate a commitment to the noble pursuit of making the American Dream more fully achievable for its own people. It would reduce the profits available for growth, but it would restore some balance between adequately compensating its people and its current obsessive expansion into every small town, megapolis, suburb, and city.

Better-paid employees and a greater focus on development and welfare would undoubtedly improve floor customer service by orders of magnitude. What customer would question Wal-Mart's need to dramatically ratchet up its overall customer-service focus? The comparison, for example, of Wal-Mart's customer service with Home Depot, Wegmans, Best Buy, or other big box retailers is striking. It is always difficult to find assistance on the floor of a Wal-Mart. Wal-Mart has given America the wonderful gift of low prices. It must now make whole its own people.

In summary, the foundational leader, as difficult as it may be, must come to realize its own people are its most important product. He or she must undergo a metamorphosis to a new paradigm of leadership. Just as our founding fathers did, they must see their mission as that of building the dream of freedom for their people, using legendary products and services as the tools for this work. The founding fathers, for the first time in history, saw the individual citizen as the primary customer and not the government. They knew that if they focused on the life, liberty, and pursuit of happiness of the individual, those individuals would collectively create an economy that could compete globally and provide adequate revenues to operate the government.

However, this paradigm is not to be confused with paternalism, which only destroys individual initiative. Today's government leaders seem to have lost sight of their mission to provide the opportunity for the individual to achieve the American Dream and to incentivize entrepreneurship—not to engage in it with deficit spending. With now almost 60 percent of all Americans receiving some kind of government entitlement, job creation has plunged, the size of government has ballooned, and the American Dream is in grave jeopardy for our younger generation. This trend has to be reversed.

Today's business leaders must return to the foundational leadership paradigm, reject obscene salaries and perks, abandon paper entrepreneurship, and dedicate themselves to building the dream of freedom for their people.

CHAPTER 8
The New Business Economics

We must move from the traditional microeconomics of the nominal to those of the maximization of business financial performance.

With such idealistic new paradigms for business enterprise, the question arises of whether these new approaches are economically feasible. What, specifically, are the microeconomics of developmentship? Can a business make a profit while pursuing the dream of freedom for its people? And aren't the current paradigms working? After all, there is currently a new wave of corporate profitability and impressive corporate turnarounds using the old leadership paradigms of merging, downsizing, cost cutting, and eliminating or exporting American jobs. Admittedly, the old paradigms do work if the goal is profitability without regard to job retention and creation and the potential for people to achieve the American Dream.

Whereas conventional theory treats individuals primarily as labor input in a production function, the paradigm of developmentship is a leadership strategy calculated to improve individual motivation and creativity—to fully develop the worker's intellectual capital. This conception takes seriously the arguments of utility maximization and choice as they relate to the individual. The basic model of choice that economists use assumes that individuals act to maximize their own best interests, while the firm chooses to maximize profits and return on investment.

When firms have made it their business to maximize people development rather than profits, productivity gains have been shown to lead to higher profits than with the classic, profit-driven model. The SAS software company is one example of the success of this paradigm. Gains that result from human capital improvements have resulted from the psychic realization (increased utility) that leadership cares for its workers.

As worker development produces reciprocal loyalty, workers have made the firm's interests their own. SAS dominates in its field and has experienced annual revenue growth for the past fifteen years, and been consistently profitable for many years, lending strong credibility to the people-centered leadership focus.

Other examples of the people first (developmentship) paradigm are Oticon, Eastman Johnsonville Foods, the Canadian Imperial Bank of Commerce, W. L. Gore, Semco, and Williams Technologies. These firms have journeyed down the path of the developmentship paradigm, and each has demonstrated the economic viability of the practice over the long haul.

Oticon, for example, tripled its return on sales, increased sales growth to 14 percent from 3 percent, reduced time to market by 50 percent, and dramatically increased new product launches in a declining market, soon after moving to the developmentship paradigm in 1993. All of the other mentioned companies have experienced similar results to the bottom line over extended intervals during both growth and contracting market cycles. Indeed, the developmentship approach appears to be the only viable strategy for ensuring continued growth and profits during recessions and negative business cycles.

In the microeconomic sense, the developmentship hypothesis rests on the premise that the worker is the greatest capital of the firm; hence, developmental leadership, by maximizing the utility of the firm's associates, has, almost invariably, realized greater economic returns. Swedish engineering firms that studied at length the influence of humanistic factors on corporate financial results have also borne out the fact that when human capital development is maximized, profits are also maximized.

The economics of developing human capital, the work of developmentship then, implies that firms should maximize the marginal productivity of each associate (by means of utility maximization), rather than profits. Investments in personnel training and intensive efforts by the leadership to mine the massive innovative potential of its people logically follow. Leadership focus shifts from mergers and acquisitions to innovating from within and creating new markets, a strategy Gifford Pinchott calls *Intraprenuering.*

The conventional objective function, profits, requires a cost-minimizing approach toward the labor input. But people have been shown to produce more when they sense that they are the product rather than agents of expendability and instrumentality. By respecifying labor as an output, rather than an input, firms can indirectly maximize profits by unleashing an enormous reservoir of previously untapped human capital.

More will be said later on using economic utility theory to design performance-maximizing compensation systems. In the meantime, let us introduce new business economic functions for maximizing revenues, production, and profits. Business microeconomics have for too long, resided in the esoteric realm of statisticians and economists, virtually incomprehensive to the leadership of business organizations.

And while there is a place for the financial analyst in the organization, executives must take the lead in translating mission, vision, and values into the hard science of navigating the global economy. More specifically, the leadership must come to a deep understanding of the economics of focusing most of their efforts on unleashing human potential and providing the conditions for the front-line people to be turned loose in cutting costs, reinventing the industry, and maximizing market share, customer satisfaction, and profits. They must move from paper entrepreneurship to developmentship.

The Hard Science of Developmentship

$$\text{IRC} = \frac{\text{Individual Salary}}{\text{Total Salaries}} \times \frac{\text{Individual Score}}{\text{Standard of Excellence}} \times \text{TR}_n$$

where,

IRC = Individual Revenue Contribution
TR_n = Total Nominal Revenues (from existing products)

(See chapter 12 for Performance Standards and Measures)

$$[\sum\text{TR}_n + \sum\text{TIR} + \sum\text{TCR}] - \text{TC} = \pi_{max}$$

where,

TIR = Team Innovation Revenues (from new products)
TCR = Team Cost Reductions (from gainsharing activities)
TC = Total Costs
π_{max} = Profit Maximization

Profit maximization occurs when productivity improvements from standards, measures, and real-time feedback on performance are channeled into team innovation and cost reductions, rather than being used as a basis for layoffs.

Maximizing corporate performance requires maximizing the growth potential with additional revenues from new products created from within, continuous cost reductions from team gainsharing initiatives, and innovation and additional revenues from selective acquisitions. Annual revenues from new products should be near

25 percent—and around 10 percent from acquisitions. Following are representations of how Q (production) and M (marketing) are maximized, and when coupled with profit maximization π_{max}, achieve corporate financial maximization.

$$R_{max} = f\,[R_n + (P \rightarrow I) + R_{acq}]$$

where,

R_{max} = Revenue Growth Maximization, R_n = Nominal Revenues P = Productivity Improvements, I = Revenues from Innovation, and R_{acq} = Revenues from Acquisitions

$$M_{max} = f\,[(S_p + DC_{op} + AP_{ex}), M_{dis}]$$

where,

M_{max} = Market Maximization, S_p = Market Segmentation Precision, DC_{op} = Distribution Channel Optimization, AP_{ex} = Advertising and Promotional Excellence, and M_{dis} = Market Disruption Factor (the reinvention of a product or service, resulting in word of mouth critical mass, where *almost everyone* feels as if they have to have the product).

$$Q_{max} = f\,(L^n + K_{max})$$

where,

Q_{max} = Production Maximization, L^n = The Releasing of the Full Productive and Innovative Potential of the People with Standards and Measures, Structured Synergy, and Gainsharing Cost Reduction, and K_{max} = The Maximization of Capital Usage through Enterprise Developer Derivations (See chapter 14.)

Just as America achieved economic dominance by providing an environment for the maximum actualization of human potential, so will the corporation actualize its potential when it places the development of its people as its highest priority and purpose.

When leaders begin to unleash the hidden potential of their people to reinvent their industries—instead of submitting to the strategy of downsizing and exporting jobs—America will again begin to create the millions of new jobs we must have to guarantee that our children have at least as good a standard of living as we enjoyed.

But we cannot achieve this new industrial miracle with archaic business paradigms. We must recognize that the electronic and communications revolutions must be accompanied by a revolution in leadership technology and behavioral science.

We must move away from the nominal business economic formulas of the past to the maximizing economics of the new organizational science.

Traditional Profit Maximization

Traditional profit maximization involves increasing p (price), q (quantity), and/or improving productivity by office automation and the reduction of costs primarily by the reduction of staff (downsizing).

The Traditional Approach to Profit Improvement

TR = Total Revenue
TC = Total Cost
q = Quantity
p = Price
π = Profit

$$TR - TC = \pi$$

qxp

Automate; Reduce People Costs by layoffs, or exporting jobs

Increase Quantity, Price, or Both

The new business economics make possible individual and team profit centers throughout the organization. The full power of the individual and the team is released as the goals of the organization merge in complete unity with the individual's goals.

Pay can be objectively tied to revenue production by individuals and teams, resulting in the maximum compensation of individuals and the maximization of profit for the organization. The new paradigm is to use profit and organizational maximization to build people. This new paradigm is win-win for all of the organization's stakeholders.

CHAPTER 9
Revisiting Compensation

*$E=nC^2$ is the universal performance-maximization
formula. Using ecomomic utility theory and this
formula, the compensation strategy can be transformed
to maximize performance in the workplace.*

For far too long, there has not been a corporate compensation strategy
that maximizes worker performance. In most cases, salaries are not
very well tied to performance, and when there are rewards for high
performance, those rewards are often based on very subjective annual
appraisals of individual workers and not on team achievement of
results. As a result, teamwork, so vital to innovation, is not well
fostered by most compensation systems.

The Universal Performance-Maximization Formula

The uranium atom is a relatively simple atom. But when enriched
in a concentrating diffusion process, it becomes capable of releasing
enormous amounts of energy. Albert Einstein, after years of study
and in an amazing stroke of brilliance, quantified the energy released

in a nuclear chain reaction or fission process with the formula $E = mC^2$, where E stands for the energy released, m represents the mass of uranium, and C represents the speed of light.

Human intelligence, when enriched with education, training, ennobling values, and lofty vision, also possesses enormous hidden power. While splitting an atom requires bombardment by neutrons, human potential is released by imbuing it with real-time feedback on performance and a similarly real-time realization of the economic utility of peak performance in the workplace. Mediocrity generally reigns in the workplace today because of the lack of real-time feedback on performance and an embedded disconnect between the economic reward system and one's performance.

The formula for unleashing this hidden potential is $E = mC^2$, where E represents extraordinary performance, m represents measurement of both work-process adherence and results on a near real-time basis, and C represents the economic cost of failure to achieve weekly process excellence and monthly financial and/or customer-satisfaction index targets (these two costs being, C^2).

Earlier, I discussed the importance of the proper application of economic utility theory. It is now time to explain in detail how this theory can be used to, for the first time, maximize the motivational power of a company's compensation system.

A free-market economy operates on the theory that all rational people are seeking to maximize personal happiness at the least possible cost because we all have budget constraints. The currency of this pursuit of happiness is fungible money. Our marginal consumption and spending decisions are based on our perception of how much utility our decision has in our quest for happiness.

The wellspring of desire is found in our sense of personal and career mission—and in our intense desire to make consumption decisions that maximize our quality of life. Paradoxically, more powerful desire emanates from our effort to wisely utilize and avoid unnecessary debits to our *existing* reservoir of fungible resources than accrues from our hope of future earnings with their imagined future economic utility.

That is why we will often expend more effort, for example, to recover an overcharge on a given purchase than we spent in seeking out the best price of our desired purchase. We have an intense desire to conserve our current fungible resources, perceiving future utility as an ideal to strive for over the long haul. The existence within the American worker of both abundant idealism *and* economic expediency enables tapping fully into the wellsprings of desire.

Another key factor in economic utility theory is what is called *time preference.* Our time preferences place a heavy value on the immediate benefit we perceive from our decisions. For example, one might love eating for pleasure and at the same time have a strong desire to lose weight. If the pleasure derived from the immediate gratification of a chocolate sundae seems to have an economic cost *less* than that of the eventual economic cost of gaining more weight, one will sacrifice the future benefit for the immediate gratification.

This behavior is influenced also by another factor in human psychology: *risk tolerance.* There are three general types of consumers: risk averse, risk neutral, and risk happy. A heavily risk-averse person generally avoids health destructive behaviors and maintains his or her ideal weight. A risk-neutral person, upon becoming overweight, can usually achieve weight loss with any number of the wonderful weight loss programs that are available.

A risk-happy person will continue, however, to engage in weight-gaining eating behaviors regardless of the almost certain long-term damage to health and happiness and regardless of how wonderful a weight loss program he or she tries—that is, *unless* an immediate economic cost is established that is greater that he or she is willing to pay. An obvious economic cost that might preclude even a risk-happy person from eating the sundae would be a price for the sundae of, let's say, ten dollars. At some point, the cost of this kind of consumption, for a rational person, is simply more than one is willing to pay.

Having now identified the major elements of economic utility theory, the expression for maximizing productive behavior can be represented by Einstein's formula:

$$E = mC^2$$

Extraordinary performance = measurement, real-time of both process and results xCost of failure at process adherence xCost of failure to achieve targeted results

A performance-maximizing compensation strategy addresses all of the principles of Statistical Process Control and economic utility theory. Process definition and real-time measurement are put in place, and bonus pools are established at the beginning of quarterly bonus payout intervals. These bonus pools are assumed to have already been earned. Teams then strive to achieve extraordinary results, using a well-defined, quality-enhancing process, in order to preclude the loss of any part of the bonus funds.

The reason this process works to generate maximizing performance is that the preexisting bonus monies represent already earned economic utility that can be lost by failure to maximize performance, rather than as incentives that are perceived as future potential rewards or icing on the cake. One's quality of life will, for most people, be geared to the maximum, currently available economic utility (one's regular salary plus the preexistent bonus monies). For obvious reasons, extraordinary effort will be expended to maintain this utility.

The formula for this compensation strategy turns out to be as sublimely simple and tremendously powerful as Einstein's formula for the astounding power that is released in a nuclear chain reaction. The beauty of it, however, is that it has none of the harmful radiation of a nuclear reaction. It is universally applicable, and its by-products are all beneficial—with the possible exception that it can result in excessive preoccupation with work if it is not moderated by sabbaticals and occasional, compensated off days for people in the peak-performance environment that results from its use.

An example of the power of this compensation strategy is Edwards Jones Company, consistently in the top ten of Fortune 500's 100 best places to work. New members are allotted a potential $50,000 initial annual salary. Stringent training and contacting requirements are established for precluding the incremental loss of this reservoir of economic utility as the year progresses. An associate typically will gear his or her lifestyle on the availability of the total potential compensation and will really work hard to avoid losing any portion of the potential, first-year income.

This strategy's motivational power is no small factor in the high achieving record and high job satisfaction of Edward Jones associates. While it does elicit maximum effort in the early years, as is always the case, for example, in priming a pump, the rewards flow richly with less effort once the pump is primed and the years go by.

Unfortunately, because economic utility theory is not generally well understood by personnel managers and finance people, this strategy has not been used widely in business, and its enormous motivational potential is still waiting to be discovered. Once implemented, however, productivity in the white-collar environment can increase by 100 percent or more.

CHAPTER 10
Reinventing Business Education

"What data there are suggest that business schools are not very effective: Neither possessing an MBA degree nor grades earned in courses correlate with career success, results that question the effectiveness of schools in preparing their students."
—Jeffery Pfeffer

Traditionally, the teaching of business administration has consisted of courses in the various business disciplines, such as finance, economics, statistics, behavioral science, etc., and the use of case studies, simulations, and other methods for teaching the application of the principles. But without an integrated theory and model of business, students have not gained an understanding of the interrelationship of the disciplines, the hierarchical dynamics of a business organization, or the balance that is essential for enduring competitiveness in a global economy.

In their classic, *In Search of Excellence,* Peters and Waterman highlighted this problem and accurately predicted that, without new business theory, future business leaders would undoubtedly flounder in an ever-increasingly competitive and complex global economy. With the failures of Enron, WorldCom, Global Crossing, Tyco, GM, and others—and the decline of former market leaders such as K-Mart, Sears, the venerable Levi Strauss, and many others—it is apparent that their predictions have come true.

It is essential that a new method and new tools for teaching business administration come forth to augment the existing approaches. With the integrated theory of business and the DSL model introduced in this work, one such approach is now possible. That approach is the *derivational approach*. The strength of the derivational approach to the teaching of disciplines has long been recognized. When given a model and a challenge to derive solutions, students must dig more deeply, calling forth solutions from within—solutions that are, as a result, internalized and *owned* by the student.

When applied in a team environment, the synergy that develops from the derivational process has enormous potential. Not only are high-quality solutions to business problems quickly identified, the realization of the importance of teamwork and the use of the derivational approach is heightened by confronting the complex issues of a turbulent environment. And this comprehensive, holistic, and synergistic approach to business can produce the balance that is essential to sustained leadership in a global economy.

In deriving an integrated theory of business, a new business discipline emerged and came clearly into focus. That new discipline is called developmentship. It is the crowning discipline in a hierarchy of disciplines. Innovation also clearly emerged as a distinct business discipline, characterized in the model as the dynamic, *the daring to innovate*. The discipline of entrepreneurial leadership, which is at the foundation of any successful business endeavor, became the *dream of freedom*.

Courses and curricula in business can now be based from the very beginning on an integrated understanding of the determinants of global competitiveness and the dynamics of business leadership and administration. Indeed, students should be introduced from the outset to an integrated business model and then engaged as a central part of their education in doing the hard mental work of deriving business essentials. Derivational work presupposes and requires serious research and synergy. While the DSL model is a first in the introduction of the derivational approach to teaching business, it is certainly only a beginning, with many other derivational approaches sure to emerge. But the derivational approach must become an essential strategy for teaching business essentials for the twenty-first-century business.

What were formerly separate, unconnected disciplines, with the integrated approach, now become interrelated, complementary, and interdependent dynamics. For example, under the determinant of *winds of change*, the essentials of coping with sea changes in the competitive environment clearly come into focus, empowering the organization to prepare for these inevitable changes in the marketplace. Derivations of the essentials of these changes include *strengthening corporate presence in foreign markets, statistical modeling of market dynamics, survey of new technologies in the industry, striving to achieve strategic breakthroughs, structural changes to adapt to competitive pressure, strong lobbying presence at high levels,* and *selection of new business partners.* The elements for coping with each of these essentials would then be derived and objectives for coping with these changes established.

Likewise, the discipline of marketing would become part of the *oceans of opportunity.* Again, a holistic, balanced, and comprehensive approach to marketing would be derived using the DSL model. Students assigned to do this derivational work would necessarily have to engage in intensive research of the literature and would be required to substantiate the derived solutions with case studies and business stories. The result would be an integration of the contingency (application of a specific discipline to a real or hypothetical business situation), the case study, and the derivational methods of instruction.

It is obvious that these and other new and more effective ways of teaching business must be implemented if the need for a holistic and balanced approach to leading a business and administering business disciplines in a supercompetitive, global economy is to be met. Barring such innovations in business academia, we are almost certain to see more implosions, declines, and tragic failures of once-great businesses and the disappearance of millions more of our jobs.

A New Way to Teach Business

- Begin the curriculum by introducing the student to the Seven Determinants of Global Competitiveness, an integrated, holistic, and comprehensive model of business.
- Lead the students sequentially through the formation of a business from the ground up by constructing the Development Ship and raising its sails one by one.
- Having identified the hierarchal business dynamics (the disciplines of business), have the students derive the essentials of these disciplines using the DSL model.
- Treat each discipline in detail in separate courses in which the elements of each dynamic and essential are derived with the DSL model.
- Have the students substantiate the derived essentials and elements of business with case studies, simulations, etc.
- Culminate the curriculum by requiring students to create a hypothetical business in a global economy, involving all the determinants, dynamics, and essentials of the business.

CHAPTER 11
Developmentship—The Bill Murff Story

In my quest to validate power of foundational leadership and the developmentship paradigm, I found rich soil in Murff's Turf Farm, near Crosby, Texas, founded by my brother, Bill. Because of Bill's extraordinary application of the principles of developmentship and his resulting notable business success, I believe today's business leaders would do well to emulate many of Bill's business practices.

In speaking of foundational leadership, America's founding fathers established an economic paradigm of power unsurpassed in the history of mankind. The American experience has demonstrated that focusing upon liberating and developing human potential (life, liberty, and the pursuit of happiness) rather than upon national economics is the great economic performance paradox. This first-of-its-kind governing system resulted in a largely undeveloped new nation quickly becoming the world's leading economy.

During a full-time, four-month study of Bill's operation and business practices—and using one facet of my model DSL (alliteration), I have identified twenty-seven essentials of what I am calling *foundational leadership* in business.

In this appendix, I will outline these essentials and relate some anecdotes from my brother's life, about his philosophy and practice and how they contribute to the maximizing of business performance.

Murff's Turf has always been profitable, even in negative business cycles and since the housing bubble burst, even though housing starts almost came to a standstill. From fifteen acres, the farm has grown to more than three thousand acres, involving both sod farming and land sales and development.

Following are some of the lessons I learned about foundational leadership and maximizing business performance from my brother and the farm:

1) Systematically Practice the Golden Rule

The Golden Rule is the universal principle for garnering respect from others. Bill's land acquisitions are a study in the validity of the golden rule and the power of giving to others more than is necessary. Bill always tried to go the extra mile in assuring that people he purchased from got a fair deal. Whereas, the typical purchaser is concerned primarily and often solely in maximizing his own advantage, Bill has always put the seller's interests ahead of his own. One such seller was a family by the name of Brown who had bought a sixty-five-acre plot of ground, only to see land values drop dramatically and had gotten into a position of imminent default on their mortgage.

Knowing of Bill's reputation for integrity and his commitment to beautifying and improving his land holdings, the Browns approached him with the proposition that he take over ownership of their land simply by assuming the mortgage payments. To Bill, this offer seemed too generous in that no equity payment was being requested. He indicated to the Browns that he would be happy to take over the land purchase, but he believed they deserved some consideration for their equity in the land. His offer to them was that they could retain the option to repurchase half the property at some future date—and that if Bill subsequently sold all or part of the property at a profit, he would split any gains realized on the sale with them.

Some years later, some of the land was purchased at a substantial profit by the local power company. True to his word, Bill immediately went to the Browns with a $100,000 check, which represented exactly half the profit on the sale. This kind of consideration for others and generosity on his part has, of course, has brought great respect from his neighbors and others that do business with him. The important principle is that equity and fairness to others in business transactions are more important than always trying to maximize short-term gains. In the long run, this kind of reputation pays off far more than any immediate advantage that might be realized by a strictly short-term, profit-driven approach and must be central to the competitive twenty-first-century business philosophy.

Several of Bill's other land transactions illustrate the true meaning of the golden rule. In one instance, a couple bought several acres of land that Bill financed. For several years, they made their payments faithfully, but then they stopped making payments altogether. After several months of no payments, Bill contacted them; it was obvious they did not want to continue the contract. Bill would have been both legally and ethically justified in initiating foreclosure procedures and could have easily gotten the property back for a minor attorney's fee. But in considering the fact that they had paid a considerably amount on the property, he felt that they deserved some consideration for this investment. He offered them a generous sum of money to compensate them should they want to voluntarily forfeit the land. They cheerfully accepted and felt as though their investment had not been a complete loss because they had been treated with true integrity.

On another occasion, a man bought a number of acres and initially demonstrated a great deal of interest in the land, eventually seeding it with Bermuda grass. Without irrigation and with a dry summer, the seed did not germinate. Bill noticed that the man was showing less and less interest in the land, seldom coming to the property. In the meantime, Bill was having an adjacent piece of property plowed up for the planting of grass, and the person doing the plowing also mistakenly plowed up the other man's land. When the man discovered the mistake, he indicated that he had suffered loss because his seeding had been undone. While the man agreed with Bill that his seeding had failed prior to the plowing, Bill nonetheless agreed to replant the property at considerable expense—with grass plugs instead of seed, a superior method of planting grass. But the man had completely lost interest in the land, and as with the previous couple, Bill offered him a generous sum of money should he want to void the contract, which he gladly accepted.

On every occasion, when foreclosure seemed appropriate upon default, Bill has shown consideration for people's investment, has given them generous reimbursements, and has avoided foreclosure procedures that alienate people and appear to make their interests subordinate to legalities.

Because of the ever-growing demand for sod, numerous other entrepreneurs also eventually entered the sod business, including the Anheuser-Busch Corporation, which moved in almost on top of Murff's Turf. But without ever spending a cent on commercial advertising, Murff's Turf Farms endured, prospered, and continued to expand, year after year, while seeing Anheuser-Busch and many other of his competitors fall by the wayside. Bill even spun off numerous competitors from his own workforce and continued to prosper.

Much of the credit for this enduring success, I believe, was Bill's perception that he was not in the sod business, but rather in the business of building the dream of freedom for his own people, and giving his customers a feeling they had never experienced before in a business transaction. This feeling was the same kind of *feel-good feeling* upon which Debbie Fields had built her cookie empire. To her associates, of which I was one for a while, Debbie often said, "I never viewed myself as being in the cookie business. I was just using my cookies and my stores to give people a feel-good feeling, a feeling as if they had just left their mom's kitchen."

Bill's approach to a business transaction is truly unique. In fact, most of his sales do not even start out as intended business transactions at all. He constantly seeks out people with which to interact, as does any great businessman. But Bill's motivation almost never involves attempting to make a sale. He is trying to find out what is unique about the individual with whom he is dealing. He simply finds joy in discovering the values and the goodness of the people with whom he meets. He learns as much as possible about the individual and genuinely seeks to find some way in which he might serve that person. He is always building America by seeking to cultivate values, build integrity, foster goodness, and share his deep love for his country and his community.

During my visits over the years Bill has invited me to ride around the farm with him. On almost every occasion, we have encountered someone Bill had never met before. Sometimes these people were trespassing—sometimes even in the act of dumping trash on his property. But Bill never employed a punitive approach to such conduct. Rather, treating the culprit with dignity and respect, he would coach the person and gain their respect, most of the time making a friend or closing a deal. A number of building lots he sold resulted from encounters with trespassers.

Bill has been a great example of true integrity to those around him and his customers. He believes that treating people fairly goes much deeper than abiding by the letter of the law. It involves going beyond the letter to make people feel as if they have been considered more important than profit or contract provisions. It requires the application of the golden rule in all dealings with people—whether employees, customers, or members of the general public. Bill's land transactions, returns in customer loyalty, and unsolicited new business have abundantly demonstrated the power of going the second mile, in treating people fairly, in putting people ahead of profits and personal advantage.

2) See Your Business as the Business of America

From his own parents' example, Bill knew that he was in the business of building a better America and that the best way to build a better America would be make the purpose of his life and that of building the dream of freedom for himself and for as many other people as possible. One of his values was hard work, and in addition to service to his family, his community, and his students during his early years as a high school agriculture teacher, he acquired a small herd of cattle and began to do small landscaping jobs around the area.

Bill had already developed a deep love of people—of young people as a teacher and of older people for their wisdom and their life stories—from whom he intended to glean the insights and expertise needed to build his American Dream out of Texas soil. It was this interest in people and willingness to listen and learn from others that led Bill into the sod business. One of these friends, a grass supplier for his landscaping job, shared with Bill his knowledge of the sod business. After calculating, based on what he was paying his friend, that he could make far more money with sod than with cattle, Bill quickly sold the cattle and planted his fifteen acres in St. Augustine grass.

With eight feet of topsoil, it was evident to Bill that his fifteen acres would yield an almost perpetual source of income—and with a great deal less trouble than with cattle. So, in 1960, he sold his first trailer load of sod. At the time, Bill could never have imagined that over the next thirty years, more than fifty thousand homes would be built near his farm in suburbs north of Houston, along with countless schools, athletic fields, and businesses, providing an almost unending demand for sod.

It took Bill four years to produce his first crop of sod. With his highly people-centered approach, it did not take long for him to find a market for his sod. It was simply a matter of doing what he enjoyed most: driving around and talking to people. Inevitably, the talk would turn to what business Bill was in, and the sales flowed naturally and effortlessly from these interactions. With the purchase of a small hand sod cutter and a pickup, he was on his way. New land acquisitions soon followed the success of marketing the first fifteen acres of sod. His slogan became: "Don't wait to buy land. Buy land and wait."

From the beginning, Bill's philosophy was to serve and develop people and help them achieve their dreams. He knew that this was the business of America, and it was going to be his fundamental business purpose.

3) Structure the Business Concentrically

A testament to the poverty of the literature on organization structure is the fact that, for almost a hundred years, we have used the pyramid as our model of the organization. Some have finally inverted the pyramid to show the leadership at the bottom, but still we think of organizations as vertical in nature.

When Henri Fayol first advanced the pyramid as the model for organizations in *General and Industrial Management,* he emphasized *planks*, linking parallel departments and divisions together. But somewhere along the way, we lost the planks; for a long time, organizations operated as isolated functional departments; marketing was not interfacing with design, and design seldom talking to manufacturing, etc.

Many other overly simplistic and equally dysfunctional models have been suggested, but the pyramid has, in reality, always won out. Even with federal decentralization, conceived by Alfred P. Sloan and practiced by the modern, large corporation, we have continued to illustrate its structure with the pyramid.

What is the right model for organization structure? I believe the answer can be observed in the structure our universe. This structure and the structure in all of matter is concentric—from galaxies down to atom. And when our founding fathers structured our government, it was as a concentric republic, the federal government in the center with the states revolving around it, self-directed but held in orbit by its gravitational pull.

I saw this principle at work immediately upon my arrival at Murff's Turf Farms. I tried to determine what the organizational structure was, and I found that there was no formal structure. People were pretty autonomous, but all were influenced by Bill's leadership and values. Everything revolved around Bill, but he did not really run anything directly. We talked a long time about adding some vertical structure and decided that things would be better left as they were—a concentric organization rotating around the leadership center.

In chapter 4, I suggest that the right way to depict the structure of American business is in the form of our solar system. The leadership is in the center—not at the top or the bottom. The orbiting systems are the business units, divisions, departments, sections, and teams. The organization is governed by a constitution and a set of values. People are empowered to act in all ways in harmony with this constitution—and with as little interference as possible.

At Murff's Turf Farms, we set out to develop a constitution for the organization that included the identification of our mission, a singular vision, a set of well-defined values, some strategic objectives, a slogan, a symbol, and a song. Having experienced rain for the entire first month I was at the farm, Keith Whitley's *I'm No Stranger to the Rain* quickly came to mind as an appropriate song.

I believe that every organization has a division or a department that is in many ways like one of the planets of our solar system. But, since a name like Jupiter or Pluto did not seem appropriate for a sod field, we decided to stick with names like the Brown Field, the Bugg Field, and one which Bill had leased to a radio controlled airplane club, called the Prop Nuts field after the name of the club.

Before I learned about the model airplane club, every time I heard the name of the field mentioned, all I could visualize was some kind of nuts that must have been growing on the field. I thought they were saying "crop nuts" for a long time and was too embarrassed to ask what they were really saying. Inasmuch as I had had a great uncle that had cultivated over many years, a new kind of sweet potato, called the Murff Bush Sweet Potato, I thought maybe Bill's highly innovative staff had cultivated a new nut that grew on a bush.

Finally, I learned that the field was leased by a model airplane club. But then, I thought that they were just making fun of the modelers. Eventually, I approached one of the model airplane club members and learned that the name of their club really was Prop Nuts. In any case, I believed that there was some merit to naming business units and divisions after planets. One of what I had come to believe was one of the most enlightened of modern day businesses, and one whose corporate culture I believed to be worthy of serving as an archetype of the twenty-first-century manufacturing concern, was the Saturn Motor Company. The company is now defunct, and I no longer believe that naming divisions after planets is a good idea. Ford's Mercury Division is also now being closed. Additionally, it occurred to me that Uranus would probably not go over well as the name of a business unit.

I point out many of the analogies between our solar system and business organizations in chapter 3, and such a conception of the business organization has great possibilities for improving the development of organizational resources. The twenty-first-century organization will benefit greatly from structuring itself in the form of our solar system. Just as the world was revolutionized by the eventual discovery that the earth revolved around the sun and was not the center of the universe, revolutionary business changes can result in the discovery that the leadership resides at the center of the organization.

Such revolutionary improvements in organization structure would involve new systems thinking as advocated by Peter Senge in *The Fifth Discipline*. Spherical structure would also nurture the organizational synergy that has been envisioned by Steven Covey in *Principled Centered Leadership*. Greater organizational interdependence and genuine, developmental communications between the leadership and the people might be another spin off of this dramatic new corporate mindset. But only when this paradigm shift actually occurs will we know what great new corporate possibilities will derive from this realization. Only now, long after having been freed from Copernican thinking, are we finally discovering unimagined distant galaxies with the Hubble telescope. Who knows what business frontiers await us as we fundamentally change the way we perceive the purposes, structure, and work of organizations.

4) Synthesize Business and Family Values

The successful twenty-first-century business will have to work hard to harmonize business and family values. Good people will seek out family-oriented businesses, and increasingly, people will seek an environment of *high touch* along with the *high tech*, as pointed out in John Naisbett's *Megatrends* more than two decades ago.

In 1939, Dow, already a prominent Michigan chemical company, began construction of a plant to extract magnesium from seawater near Freeport, Texas. Like many dirt-poor farmers, my father moved from central Texas to work for Dow. From the very first, with its Texas operations, Dow saw itself in the business of building families and communities as well as making profits and preserving America's freedom with its contribution to the war effort. Dow found a thousand ways to serve the families that had come to work there and the new communities that it spawned in the area. I was a product of Dow's interest in its people, having been treated in its hospitals, provided for by its excellent wages to my father, enjoyed the parks it had created, and in many other ways.

In addition to the living it provided for my family, Dow provided me with summer employment while I was attending Texas A&M University, granted scholarships for many local students, and vigorously supported the schools in the area. Dow built hospitals, community centers, ballparks, and an entire model city—Lake Jackson, Texas—in the former swamps and forests of the undeveloped portion of the Gulf Coast in that region.

When my father retired at the age of fifty-six after twenty-six years of service, his monthly retirement sum was relatively low because of his early departure. But over the years, Dow voluntarily increased his monthly pension several times and provided paid-up life insurance, which it also increased in value as the value of the dollar decreased. The company still holds an annual barbecue and reunion for all retired personnel of the Texas operations. The company has continued to care about its people long after they have departed.

It was not surprising when I attended the Texas Barbecue Cook-off at the Astrodome some years ago, that Dow's was the only one that was open to the public—out of 327 booths. The company's love of people radiated from every one of the Dow employees as they served the finest barbecue, crawfish etouffee, and all of the trimmings, free of charge, all you could eat, to anyone who came in. I saw the power of that public relations effort, when Bill stopped couple after couple and directed them to the booth with kind words about the Dow Chemical Company.

Murff's Turf Farms exemplifies that same philosophy. The company has built a small community center, has fostered high-quality homebuilding on parts of the farm, and has sought to foster the dreams of every one of its employees. One faithful employee in particular, who after eighteen years of service with the farm, which provided his family with medical insurance but with no formal retirement program, was walking on a beautiful, wooded piece of the property one day. The employee mentioned that he needed the afternoon off in order to go with his wife to look at a piece of property on which to build their retirement home.

Bill said, "Why not build your home here. I will deed you this eighteen acres as your retirement compensation, since I have not provided you with a formal retirement program." The offer was cheerfully accepted, and this mere handyman resides in a beautiful home on the land Bill gave him.

Murff's Turf Farms cares deeply about the family. The farm employs about forty hourly workers and, during the winter, there is often rainy and cold weather during which little work can be done in the fields. Bill nonetheless pays them for forty hours every week, a practice that is unheard of for hourly farm workers anywhere that I know of. He recognizes that these workers have families and the need for a steady income. Such practices obviously foster deep loyalty and dedication on the part of these hourly workers.

All of Bill's children are now working in the business, some after pursuing careers elsewhere for several years. They all have homes on the property and are committed to perpetuating the same family values upon which Murff's Turf was founded. And when I ran out of employment options at the age of fifty-eight, true to form, Bill invited me to live in a vacant home on his property and offered me employment with the business, or if I desired, to finance me in starting my own business. Bill is truly committed to family, both to his immediate family and to the families of his employees and associates.

Of course, there are many examples of businesses that have chosen to place people and family values as a very high priority; almost without exception, these businesses have survived the hard times. During the Christmas season of 1995, a textile company in Massachusetts burned to the ground, but the founder and owner chose to continue to pay his employees even though they no longer had a place to come to work. The company never stopped paying its people, and the company has now rebuilt its factory and is thriving and prospering.

Some years ago, the founders of an electronic business in California sold the business at a huge profit and chose to share the gains with their former employees. Some of the employees received multimillion-dollar bonuses, and many received bonuses of up to $75,000. It was reported that thousands of people subsequently called to inquire about employment with this company. Such business practices naturally attract the brightest and best people and will be crucial to the success of the business enterprise during the twenty-first century.

I recently watched a segment on a TV business channel about a company that allows employees to bring their newborn babies to work with them rather than having them be out of work for weeks after the birth. The program has been well received, has built a family culture at work, and appears to have little if any negative effect on productivity. Everyone seems willing—and even desirous—to pitch in with special needs of the new mother and child, and work has become more like family. The company's turnover rate has been determined to be one of the lowest in the country, largely due to the effect of this program.

In the twenty-first century, business, even the conglomerates, must become family-oriented organizations whose mission will have to be to develop the full potential of their people, to foster and preserve traditional family values, and to raise the moral standard of their people.

5) Set the Standard for Integrity

If anything characterizes my brother, Bill, it is his integrity. Integrity is at the heart of his business dealings, and it will have to be at the heart of every successful enterprise in the twenty-first century. Long before Bill founded Murff's Turf Farms, he was building a reputation for integrity. He became well known by his agriculture students at the Crosby High School for his insistence on always doing the right thing, regardless of the consequences.

His ability to inspire integrity in others was illustrated by a breach of this principle by some of his students. Bill had taken his class to a cattle auction; during the auction, three of the boys stole some items from a truck parked outside the auction barn. The next day, the owner, suspecting the students, called Bill and indicated that the items had been taken and that he believed some of his class members were responsible.

Bill confronted the class leader who had become aware of the theft, and gave him three options. He said, "Mel, you can have the culprits report to the principal, confess to their parents their misdeed, or take the items, themselves, back to their owner and apologize to him personally." When Mel took the options back to class, the guilty parties came forth, returned the items to the owner, and apologized to him. From that day forward, his students knew that they had to maintain a high standard of integrity in his class. I recently sat in the office with Bill and met Mel for the first time, some thirty years after this incident occurred. Mel had subsequently worked for a time with Bill, and I could sense the deep respect these two men still had for each other.

Some years ago, Bill decided to contract out the operation of his farm to a large Canadian sod company. He had visited the Canadian operation and had been favorably impressed; however, because of his own standard of integrity which he expected in others he did not read the contract very carefully or have an attorney read it. The contract was signed, but within three weeks, it became evident to Bill that this company did not have the standards of integrity upon which he had built his business. Sod was being sold with no payment to Bill forthcoming—and upon a close reading of the contract—without any hope of payment for a long period of time. And other breaches toward both customers and local suppliers quickly became evident. So Bill canceled the contract, ordered the company off his property, and took a $100,000 loss on the brief encounter. He lived up to the letter of the cancellation clause in the contract, swallowed the bitter pill, and quickly returned the business to the high standards of integrity and customer service upon which he had built the company. Bill's integrity is far more important to him than money.

On the other side of the coin, the Dow Corning Company, ironically, a company jointly owned by Dow Chemical and the Corning Glass Company some years ago demonstrated the devastating effect of the lack of integrity and the addiction to profits over people with the silicone breast implant fiasco. The wife of the vice president in charge of corporate ethics (in her judgment) became severely debilitated by a Dow Corning produced implant. Yet, he continued to defend the company—even in the face of his wife's conviction that the implants were gravely harming her and many other women and in spite of ever-growing evidence of the harmfulness of these implants. What had once been a greatly respected and highly profitable company was eventually forced to declare bankruptcy as a result of the ethical lapses involved in the silicone implant episode.

The A.H. Robbins Company™ (Chapstick®) was also nearly destroyed some years ago by a similar pursuit of profits over product users' welfare in the toxic shock syndrome associated with one of their products. The company continued to defend its product long after it had become evident that the product had resulted in the deaths of a number of users. Johnson & Johnson, on the other hand, has turned similar tragedies, such as the Tylenol® deaths—by their willingness to immediately acknowledge the problem and accept the losses associated with quickly pulling all such products from the market—into events that actually ended up bolstering consumer confidence in the company's integrity.

True integrity goes much deeper than abiding by the letter of the law. It involves going beyond the letter to make people feel as if they have been considered more important than mere money or contract provisions. It requires the application of the golden rule in all dealings with people—whether employees, customers, other stakeholders, or members of the general public.

Bill has consistently demonstrated the deeper meaning of integrity and his high regard for other people. At one juncture, Bill acquired a large tract of land about sixty miles away from his Crosby farms and spent a large sum of money preparing it to produce sod. This investment never did become profitable, however, and Bill eventually just gave the property away to the man who had been managing it. Still, there was about $75,000's worth of equipment on the land. The new owner called Bill one day wanting to use the equipment for collateral for a loan. Bill ended up giving him the equipment also.

This man continued to purchase occasional truckloads of sod from Bill. One day, Bill accompanied the trucker to his farm. The former associate was unloading the sod by hand, and Bill asked why he had not purchased a forklift truck, indicating that he could probably sell a great deal more sod if he could move it efficiently. The former associate indicated that he could not afford one at the time; Bill offered to buy one at a cost of $10,000 and to sell it to him a year later for $9,000 if it turned out to be a good investment for the former associate. Sure enough, his grass business dramatically improved almost immediately, and true to his word, Bill sold him the forklift truck for $9,000 a year later. Since that time, more than ten years ago, the former associate has been a steady and very substantial customer of Bill's.

Bill has, without a conscious attempt, tapped into a biblical principle. "Give, and it shall be given unto you; good measure, pressed down, and shaken together, and running over, shall men give unto your bosom" (Luke 6:38).

One day, representatives from a pipeline company came to him with proposal to run a pipeline on a piece of land Bill had already sold to the power company, which had put a high-voltage transmission line on the property. Bill indicated to the men that he no longer owned the property (he still owned the property on each side of the transmission line), but they kept insisting that they wanted to pay him for running the pipeline. He finally acceded to their desire and gladly accepted $41,000 from them. To this day, he does not understand why the pipeline company was so determined to pay him for crossing some someone else's land. But in my judgment, the law of the harvest simply had decreed that in giving to others, Bill's overall account was out of balance, and it was his time to receive.

All of this is to say that, while integrity is its own reward, it is also a great economic principle. People are attracted to men of integrity. One of Bill's choicest pieces of property was acquired by him as a result of his reputation for integrity. A former mayor of Houston had purchased a piece of property many years ago from the local school district. Over the years, he had never paid the property taxes on the land, however, and eventually, the school district repossessed the property. A sheriff's sale of the property was conducted, but no one made an offer.

Because of Bill's reputation for always paying his bills and taxes, the school district approached Bill and offered him the land for the value of the back taxes owed on the land. Bill accepted the offer, paid the taxes, and acquired the land for a fraction of its actual value.

The bottom line is that the twenty-first-century businessperson will have to rise to a new standard of integrity in order to prosper. No longer will just abiding by the letter of the law be sufficient. People will have to truly be treated with consideration, dignity, and respect. In every aspect of the business, the spirit as well as the letter of the law will have to be adhered to, and the higher principles of human conduct, the golden rule, and the law of giving will have to be part of the fabric of the enterprise in the twenty-first century.

6) Spin Off Competitors

One of the things Bill Murff has done consistently throughout his career as a businessman is to help his people start their own business if that is what they have wanted to do. He has put a number of people in the sod business and some in the trucking business; when I came to join him, he offered to put me into the barbecue business. He was willing to provide the building and all of the equipment to get me started rather than to have me working for him. He believes that people need to be doing their own thing if possible. His motivation is his genuine desire to see people succeed and realize their own dreams.

As a result of Bill's support, there are several competitors that have successful sod operations in the Crosby area. Even when his people have chosen to remain in his employ, he has allowed them to have their own plots of soil on his farm. He buys the sod from them wholesale and sells it retail. So almost everyone has some kind of personal stake in the business. His people are not only working for Murff's Turf Farms—they are also working for themselves. Their resulting loyalty and dedication is one of the secrets of the success of Murff's Turf.

Rather than fearing competition, Bill has always thrived on it. He recognizes that good competition is essential for the best to keep getting better. He has spun off a trucker that owns his own trucks and does all of Murff's Turf deliveries. He has also given this individual substantial acreage to farm. During deliveries, this individual often distributes his own business cards and promotes direct sales of grass from his fields. Bill is aware of this practice and feels absolutely unthreatened by it. He continues to sell more grass than he can grow—with very little promotion. This man is so highly motivated that grass delivery is obviously not an area of concern with Murff's Turf Farms.

Speaking of trucking, Bill told me of a chance meeting with a man by the name of Buck Buchanan some years ago. Buck was a business consultant and seminar leader, and as usual, Bill struck a deal with him to speak at the sod association of which he was an officer. During this seminar, Buck asked for a show of hands as to which of the attendees were experiencing difficulties with the trucking of their product. Almost all hands went up, and it turned out that almost all were doing their own trucking. But by allowing his trucker to operate his own business and even compete with him in the sod business, Bill was experiencing high-quality, virtually trouble-free delivery service.

The more I am around Bill, the more I come to realize that the secret of his success is the great paradox that when your number-one goal is to develop people, you can hardly escape success in business. People are so powerfully motivated by this philosophy that they become tremendously committed to making the business succeed.

One of the greatest business success stories of all time, the growth of Microsoft™ and the success of IBM™ in the PC business resulted from this philosophy. IBM's decision to license DOS™ to other PC manufacturers and allow them to compete with IBM™ brought about the PC revolution of the 1980s, and it resulted in Microsoft's almost total domination of the operating system software business. Apple™, on the other hand, which had a far superior operating system, chose to keep it to themselves and to stifle competition in order to maximize profits. As a result, Apple's operating system has a mere 5 percent of the operating systems market, with Microsoft's Windows at 89 percent.

The 3M Company™ has gained fame and great success by fostering entrepreneurs within the company and allowing them to run businesses for products they have conceived and nurtured. Almost everyone is familiar with the famous Post-It Note™ story, which began when an employee found a use for a weak glue that had been developed unintentionally by someone within 3M™. He initially used the weak glue on slips of paper to mark songs in his church hymnal in his calling as song director. Realizing that this idea might be a winner, he nurtured the product and went on to direct one of the most successful of all 3M™ businesses.

I once read of a chief executive whose number-one goal was to create millionaires out of his employees. He encouraged all of his people to create new businesses during working hours at his company. When they did, and had done their homework and committed some of their own capital, he would invest the company's funds in their ideas and spin off a new business, sometimes in direct competition.

He had already created a number of millionaires in the fashion and his company was flourishing from the tremendous entrepreneurial spirit within the company.

Bill has this same philosophy. He wants to see people become as prosperous in their own right, and he will help them all he can. Contrast this philosophy with the typical chief executive of today's large company that earns millions of dollars per year by eliminating other people's jobs and maximizing quarterly earnings. And contrast their salaries with the front-line people's salaries, often earning hundreds of times that of their people. This philosophy will not survive in the twenty-first century. Equity is a law of the universe. Balance will happen. Alignment will occur.

Executives of the twenty-first century who aggrandize themselves while readily sacrificing their people rather than tapping into their entrepreneurial potential will not survive. There is too much inherent waste in this philosophy, and the business of the twenty-first century will have to develop intellectual capital efficiently and highly creatively.

One of my career pursuits has been the solution to the white-collar productivity problem. For years, I tried to learn how to measure white-collar productivity. Only when I finally realized that with most knowledge work you cannot developmentally quantify output and that the *person* is the product, did I succeed in successfully measuring knowledge-work performance. I found that you could measure the person's own career growth and his or her customer-service process and that all of the data for this measurement system resided within the knowledge worker himself or herself at any given time. That made possible a self-measurement system for the first time of the knowledge-work process. I cover this discovery in detail in appendix II of this work.

In summary, it will become the standard in the twenty-first century that the purpose of a business is to develop people, to spin off new businesses, even competitors, and to thereby release the full, powerful potential of the human spirit. This ideal is the purpose of society, and business is simply a mechanism for bringing about this purpose—as are all other societal organizations. So the successful twenty-first-century business will have to be one in which the person is the product and his or her success is the main goal and purpose of the organization. Any other purpose is certain to render a business less competitive early in the twenty-first century.

7) Steer Clear of Business Fads

One of the most important paradigm shifts that will be required of twenty-first-century businesses will be moving away from business fads to a commitment to a holistic, integrated approach to operating a business. Billions of dollars of corporate America's investment in training has been almost completely wasted pursuing the latest business fad. First, there was all of the meaningless training that resulted from the discovery of the halo effect in the studies at Western Electric's Hawthorne Plant during the 1930s. Everything from T-groups to sensitivity sessions came out of this discovery that people need to be paid attention to and their needs addressed.

Next, there was behavior-modification training that came out of B. F. Skinner's work at Harvard University in the forties. Building on Skinner's work, Ken Blanchard made millions during the 1980s teaching managers how to praise people in hopes of getting them to repeat positive behaviors, much like training pigeons in a box to go to a lever in the opposite corner of the box, kick a lever, and then come back to the original corner. And while I loved his work as much as anyone—and used it extensively in my own career of developing people—I was somewhat disappointed to see that during an October 1997 international satellite session on shared leadership, Ken had not really moved beyond this overly simplistic approach to motivating people. He was still using the Shamu stories and the exact same melodramatic material from his 1980s *One Minute Manager* video. He and of the rest of the management gurus were still wedded to the old *management* paradigm, the *handling of people*, rather than having shifted to the twenty-first-century paradigm of *developmentship*, which is at the core of this work.

Then there were thirty years of trying to apply Drucker's management by objectives approach, first put forth in his 1950s *The Practice of Management*. In the meantime, there were scores of other fads that the consultants and business authors came up with, most of which have faded away after the initial excitement and the millions spent on training. Even when a truly valid, new approach to business, Total Quality Management, evolved out of forty years of effort by the Japanese to apply principles initially developed at the Bell laboratories and used by America to help win World War II, namely SPC (Statistical Process Control), most American businesses treated it as the latest fad and failed in its application.

I was shocked when I started studying management thirty years ago and found that the world's foremost management authority, Peter Drucker, had declined in his 1973 masterwork (see Drucker's, *Management, Tasks, Responsibilities & Practices*, p. 49) to offer an integrated theory of business. He said, "We do not yet have a genuine theory of business and no integrated discipline of business."

When Peters and Waterman published *In Search of Excellence,* they too stated the need for an integrated theory of business, but also declined to attempt one. In fact, Tom Peters, in the same October 1997 shared leadership conference mentioned previously, began his presentation by announcing that he had no *theory* of business—that he feared anyone who did have one—and after his exhaustive research over many years, he had come to the conclusion that it is simply impossible to discern what is going on in business today. It is one of the purposes of this book nonetheless, to offer just such an integrated theory of business, which I introduced in chapter 6.

Fortunately, a business like Murff's Turf Farms is spared exposure to the fads and has to operate as a holistic business, addressing each of the seven business disciplines on a continuing basis in order to survive. While Bill did not know about the *seven dynamics of developmentship* when he started his business, he was powerfully motivated by his *dream of freedom,* that of having his own business and the freedom to do what he was born to do. He had the *determination to raise capital* by foregoing certain amenities in order to generate the capital he needed to obtain his initial fifteen acres.

The next dynamic, *the drive to market,* came naturally to Bill as he drove around talking to people to find out what they needed and how he could best serve them. And he had exercised the *discipline of quality* in carefully nurturing his first crop of St. Augustine. He knew that the product had to be high quality in order to retain landscapers and gain repeat customers. So he was diligent in fertilizing, mowing, and caring for the grass fields. He drove the fields constantly and came to know the quality of every square foot of the grass. He refused to ship substandard sod. And he gained a reputation for quality that lives until this day.

Then, as his business began to grow, he was careful to never incur more debt than he knew he could service with his grass sales. He exercised *the diligence of financial control* by keeping growth closely synchronized with his ability to make his land payments and only once got into cash flow trouble.

One summer, there was a severe drought coupled with a sharp decline in grass prices, and for a year he could not make the payments on one of the large fields he had financed with the Federal Land Bank. Fortunately, however, they had already had so many defaults that year that they were not interested in repossessing this field and were willing to wait for their money. The following year, grass prices improved dramatically, rain came, and Bill was able to make both the current and past due payments to keep the land.

Bill knew that financial controls had to be implemented, and taxes had to be promptly and honestly paid. So, early on, he retained an excellent accountant to keep and watch over the books and the cash flow of the business.

Bill has only been audited by the IRS once—even though his tax bill has amounted to hundreds of thousands of dollars in recent years.

This audit revealed few problems and resulted in only a minor revision of the tax return for the audited year.

Bill's belief in people has always resulted in his practicing *the daring to innovate*, which is allowing everyone to use their creativity to continuously improve the business. He constantly solicits ideas from his people and then instructs them to go try their idea. If they fail, he celebrates the fact that they tried. And then he encourages them to try something new—until they find something that works better than the old way. Out of this philosophy have come numerous innovative, successful approaches to the sod business—some of which the prominent state universities still say will not work—and they are working nonetheless at Murff's Turf Farms.

For example, Bill uses a highly unusual way to plant St. Augustine grass. It is a homemade sprig spreader conceived and built at the Farms that can plant an entire field in record time. Bill has never sought a patent on the machine, preferring to share the idea with others in hopes they will benefit from it too. A number of other sod farmers are successfully using similar machines copied from Bill's. He views such contributions as simply repayment for all of the guidance and assistance he has received from others in building his business, much like Benjamin Franklin, who deliberately refrained from patenting any of his inventions for the same reason. When others patented and profited from Franklin's ideas—such as the revolutionary Franklin stove—Benjamin Franklin rejoiced rather than seeking a share of the profits or becoming resentful. Bill exemplifies that philosophy.

Finally, from the beginning, Bill has been *dedicated to developmentship*, recognizing his responsibility to develop the full potential of his people, to protect the environment, to support his community, and to foster the founding values of his country.

Recently, I was riding around with him, and as he typically does, he stopped to visit with a family that had purchased land from him and whose son was raising a prize steer for the next livestock show in the area. The family expressed their appreciation to Bill for being the sponsor of their son. He had contributed several hundred dollars to the local FFA for the purchase of a steer by one of the FFA members, but he had not realized the money had gone to this family.

Over the years, Bill has served on the local school board, has been active in politics, has served as president of sod associations, and has served his community in countless other ways. He recognized early that Murff's Turf Farms needed to be in harmony with the environment. At times, he has maintained a frontier mentality and used his own approaches to environmental protection rather than the county's or the state's regulations. When they have intervened and insisted that things be done their way, he has readily conformed to the regulations. But he has sometimes used the approach that it is easier to obtain forgiveness than to obtain permission when the regulations seemed out of harmony with what was actually best for the environment and with reality.

For example, when Bill decided to turn a beautiful, heavily wooded piece of property into a nice subdivision, he proceeded with the clearing, roads, power, culverts, and drainage systems for the property, which was in the flood plain, without a permit. He was fully aware that he would eventually have to obtain permits and, sure enough, one day he found a red tag on the gate instructing him to stop all further development activities until the proper permits had been obtained. He immediately retained a civil engineer to work with the county to get into compliance.

This breach came to light shortly after I arrived from Utah to live near and work with Bill. His free-spirited approach to subdividing is obviously not a viable approach in today's world, but it served to bring me to the realization that, while Bill is in many ways a role model for the twenty-first-century businessperson, he is not perfect by any means.

Bill derives his greatest joy through his *dedication to developmentship*. This dynamic is the one of the two that—when acquired and practiced—does not diminish in its motivational power. It actually increases in motivational power the more it is practiced (see chapter 5 for an explanation of this phenomenon). Bill has arrived at a point where he can spend most of his time developing people, the thing that he most loves to do and that brings him the most joy. These people include his grandchildren—all of whom love on the farm—and they idolize him. I cannot imagine how great these children are going to turn out with the nurturing and love and the work ethic they are being given by their parents and grandparents, all of whom are striving together to build a better America.

The day after I arrived at the farm, the phone rang while Bill and I were talking in my living room. It was business executive asking for advice about whether he should buy a backhoe for moving dirt around his dream home that was under construction nearby. After they talked for about half an hour, Bill advised the man what he would do. The man took his advice and rented a backhoe rather than buying one.

When Bill drove by the man's new home the next day and observed, however, that they were trying to spread dirt with a backhoe, which is not what he had thought they were going to be doing, he immediately proceeded to bring one of his own dozers to the site to spread the dirt. This kind of service is what he seems to enjoy most: finding one of his people, a neighbor, or someone else in the community that needs help and serving that person while sharing his values with them along the way and finding ways to help them fulfill their dreams.

The essence of this ground rule is that, during the twenty-first century, all seven of the dynamics of the developmentship and disciplines of business will have to be addressed simultaneously in a balanced, holistic, and reasoned approach. People will no longer tolerate the hypocritical dumping of training upon them in the latest business fad while the executives continue engaging in paper entrepreneurship and expect everyone else to revolutionize performance with some kind of clever new business idea.

8) Shed Payables, Strengthen Receivables

One of the most dysfunctional of all business practices is the delayed payment of bills. The accountants have somehow perpetrated the myth that float is more profitable than trust. And the payables department has mastered the art of delayed payment and the alienation of vendors and suppliers. Murff's Turf Farms has, on the other hand, always made it a policy to pay its bills immediately upon receipt of the goods—even when its own customers drag out payment for sixty to ninety days. As a consequence, Murff's Turf Farms is highly respected, and its suppliers are extraordinarily responsive; I believe this policy is one of the secrets of Murff's Turf Farm's enduring success.

I had personal experience as an accounts payable clerk at one company. In fact, I was fired from the company for trying to get vendors paid that had been waiting for months for their money. And I believe that the company's policy to defer payment of their bills was a significant factor in the eventual takeover of the company. While I was in the accounts payables department, we paid every bill for every major and minor purchase for 700 stores scattered all over the United States. The invoices flowed like a raging river, many of them regularly being lost in the shuffle. It was almost impossible to process all of the paper. And we often delayed payment by as long as six months, resulting in the loss of some of our best vendors who eventually refused to do any further business with the company.

In contrast to this destructive approach, the Ford Motor Company, some years ago, entirely eliminated the accounts payable department in favor of immediate payment of their bills. They established computerized purchasing links with their vendors, began allowing the vendors to initiate the orders based on the rate of consumption, and had their system generate payment immediately upon verification of delivery of the parts and supplies.

They found that the money saved from the elimination of the accounts payable department and the savings incurred from closer ties with—and the engendered trust and improved quality from—

their suppliers far exceeded what they had been earning on the float from unpaid bills. I believe that this enlightened practice will have to become the standard for twenty-first-century business as the survival of good suppliers becomes more and more critical to the success of the large enterprise.

On the other hand, the receivables department must become more adept at bringing about prompt payment for services rendered. Obviously, prompt payment of bills owed must be accompanied by timely receipt of payment for services delivered. Murff's Turf Farms has, over the years, used some innovative ways to recover payment for services rendered. On one occasion, a customer had received delivery of more than $18,000's worth of grass over a several month period, with no payment forthcoming after repeated requests for payment. Finally, Bill met with the man and, instead of using pressure tactics and threats, offered the man an expense-paid trip to Mexico with his wife if he would pay the bill. The man accepted the offer, paid the bill, and had a delightful time with his wife at a Mexican coastal resort. He became a loyal customer and subsequently promptly paid his bills.

I was amazed at the weak collection efforts of vendors at the company where I worked as a payables clerk. There was absolutely no creative thinking on the part of the vendors and no understanding of how to bring about payment of delinquent bills. Inevitably, they would refer their seriously delinquent bills to collection agencies that usually were no more successful than they were at collecting the owed money. I encountered only one vendor who knew how to get payment from this company for long overdue bills.

I got a call from a small service and repair contractor who indicated that he had obtained a court judgment against the company; if we did not have a check in his hands within three days, he would be at our store with a sheriff to disconnect and haul off our equipment. We complied with his request immediately. We paid for the services that he had rendered but refused initially to pay the $300 court costs he had incurred. Again, he threatened to haul off our equipment; again, we quickly sent a check.

While, obviously, court judgments are not the desirable way to collect for unpaid invoices, they may sometimes be necessary. But more constructive are the many creative and positive ways that can be used to speed up payment. Incentives work well with some customers, and most companies use them. But when incentives are not utilized by customers, other creative ways to collect bills can be very effective. It is not my intent to offer solutions to this problem, but merely to point out that for the twenty-first-century business, prompt payment of bills—coupled with prompt receipt of payment for services rendered—will have to become the norm in order to survive in the supercompetitive business environment that will characterize the twenty-first century.

9) Solve the White-Collar Productivity Problem

In Appendix II, I discuss the white-collar productivity problem in detail and offer solutions to this long-intractable condition. The fact is that white-collar performance can never improve without the implementation of real-time feedback on the white-collar process. Since all work is a process, and since processes cannot function efficiently without this kind of feedback, it is axiomatic that performance standards and near real-time measurement and feedback must replace the annual performance appraisal if improvement in this area is ever to be achieved. Lester Thurow, former dean of the Sloan School of Business at M.I.T. and noted authority on the white-collar productivity problem, has called this problem one of the most critical problems facing American businesses. More than 70 percent of the salaries in the United States now go to the white-collar sector; during the twenty-first century, making the knowledge worker productive is going to be one of the most important challenges for business.

Peter Drucker, who predicted almost every major business trend of the last fifty years, also called making the knowledge worker productive one of the major challenges facing the business leader of the future. There is a tremendous waste of human potential in this sector, and except in the high-tech industries, a trillion-dollar investment in office automation in the past thirty-five years, has failed to yield the needed productivity improvements.

One example of the seriousness of this problem is a study done by The Ford Motor Company that compared the administrative costs of making an automobile in Germany with those costs for the same car in the United States They found that the cost in the United States amounted to one-fifth of the cost of the automobile; in Germany, these costs amounted to only about 5 percent of the cost of the car.

At Murff's Turf real-time feedback on performance in both the office and the sod fields is generated abundantly by Bill. He spends most of his day in his pickup constantly touring and observing farm operations and making frequent visits to the office. He does not micro-manage his people. Rather, he tries to catch them doing something right with each observation and visit. He always has a positive word for his people, and constantly expresses his appreciation for their excellent service. At the same time, he frequently provides them with tips for improving the quality of the sod and constantly exemplifies legendary customer service in his interaction with the farm's customers.

This kind of informal feedback is much rarer in the office, and I spent twenty years trying to solve this problem. Finally, with the realization that the *person is the product* in the white-collar environment (blue collar as well, for that matter) I was able to devise a valid way to formally measure knowledge-worker performance on a real-time basis.

During the twenty-first century, the massive storehouse of untapped potential in the white-collar sector must be released. This challenge will require replacement of the current *personnel management* paradigm with a completely new discipline I call *developmentship*. A new metaphor of business will be required—one that is truly representative of the complexity and vitality of organizations. I describe this new discipline and introduce the new metaphor of business in chapter 2.

10) Strive to Create Beauty

.

When I moved back to Texas after thirty-five years of wandering the world—the last sixteen in Utah—I began taking four-mile walks with Bill on a remote, wooded section of the farm. He had been personally clearing, draining, and beautifying the 360 acres with his bulldozer, maintainer, and other equipment. He had created a number of ponds, planted fish in the ponds, and beautified the property in many other ways.

I asked Bill why he was doing this, and I was not surprised by his answer. He was just trying to create beauty that he hoped people could enjoy. When I asked him which people, he replied, "The future members of his planned subdivision—and anyone else that happens to wander onto the property." He does not put up fences. His land is open to all who will treat it with respect. His life is really about creating beauty.

Perhaps Bill is in the business of creating hundreds and hundreds of acres of lawns because, by doing so, he can do the two things he loves most: create beauty and help people develop their potential. My sixteen-year-old son accompanied me on my move to Texas. I soon tried to get Jesse to visit the nearby San Jacinto Monument with me. I also tried to get him to go to Galveston with me. The neighbors tried to get him to play basketball with them. We could not get him out of the house where he rotated among the pool table, the television, and the computer.

Not until Bill got him and put him on a tractor, rolling the fields of St. Augustine grass, did he gladly leave the house. Bill knew that Jesse needed meaningful work—work often lacking in the lives of youth today. Jesse reveled in it, and Bill was doing what he loves best: building a young man and creating beauty with sod. He had done a similar thing some years earlier with my older sons, David and Michael, one of whom has now become an executive chef and the other an upper executive with PayPal.

I have enjoyed the beautiful skylines of the great cities. On our way to Texas, Jesse and I drove the expressway through the heart of Dallas. Several buildings gained our admiration. One in particular, however, literally enthralled us as we saw its many facets from different angles as the freeway wound its way through the heart of the city. Obviously, those responsible for this magnificent structure were trying to create beauty and had succeeded in a marvelous way.

The important point is that we must view the twenty-first-century business much more aesthetically than we now do. Business must genuinely begin to view itself as an instrument for shaping values: honesty, family, morality, virtue, and beauty. Profit is a natural by-product of pursuing loftier goals, just as love comes to those who lose themselves in service to others rather than those who set out to be loved.

So, during the twenty-first century, it will be paramount for businesses to strive to beautify their surroundings. There are already thousands of examples of businesses that have recognized their responsibility to beautify their surroundings. They are too numerous to mention in this narrative, but in the twenty-first century, creating beauty must become a priority for every business.

11) Stop Merging

If businesses continue to merge at the current rate, by the year 2050, there will be only one company in the United States. I'm being facetious, but nonetheless, merger-mania is a real phenomenon that substitutes for genuine entrepreneurship.

Today's business leaders apparently see their jobs in terms of creating wonderful corporate marriages, rather than in terms of true entrepreneurship, which involves creating synergy with their own people, instead of constantly seeking to create synergy by another acquisition. There is somehow the erroneous notion that, in a global economy, survival hinges on size. How long will it take business leaders to learn the lesson of the dinosaurs?

Bill Murff never did try to get into the acquisition game. As I said earlier in this narrative, he chose to spin off competitors rather than acquire them. He loves good competition, and it has served him well to keep the sod business in his area healthy. Everyone has benefited, especially the consumer, and Bill is still making an excellent living and supporting a lot of people. He has never had to downsize after acquiring a new sod company because he has never acquired one. He has chosen to stay focused on what he does best. He is a true entrepreneur. He took me in, and I helped him further clarify his business vision. There is still much potential in exploiting the untapped resources within his own organization.

The key to remaining competitive is in tapping into the enormous storehouse of potential already within the company. Before I arrived, Murff's Turf Farms saw itself as being in the grass business. After a few weeks of brainstorming, however, it became clear that the business the company was really in was: "Nurturing the American Dream and Bringing Beauty to the Landscape of Life." There is much more revenue potential within the existing company than is presently being realized, but it will take a great deal more mental effort to actualize this potential than it would to simply go out and purchase the other sod companies in the area, sell off some of the assets to reduce the leverage, and then lay off people because of the new, downsized company.

The important principle is that the twenty-first-century business leader must recognize that his or her job is not to orchestrate grand synergy through the marriage of similar companies; it is to develop the full potential of their own people and to revolutionize the productivity of the workers within their organizations. By doing so, they will be benefiting their society far more than they could by creating larger mergers and leaving human casualties from the inevitable downsizing in the wake of these combinations.

12) Shape Societal Values

The business that largely made Benjamin Franklin financially independent at the age of forty-two was *Poor Richard's Almanac*, which he began publishing at the age of twenty-six. With an annual circulation of more than 10,000, it was one of his chief sources of income during his business career. And he frankly admitted that one of his primary purposes in producing the almanac was to help shape the values of an emerging nation.

Franklin scoured the world's great literature for kernels of truth to which he would offer his own twist and sprinkle them on each page of his almanac. The values of hard work, honesty, friendship, virtue, and all of the other values that must be at the core of a free and productive society were perpetrated at a time when the almanac was, with the exception of the Bible, the most popular publication and one of the only nationally distributed publications in America.

When Murff's Turf Farms finally began to use commercial advertising after thirty years without any advertising at all, it was with this same idea in mind. Bill wanted to promote traditional values in his advertising. So he chose a conversational radio format on a daily garden show during which the hosts of the show who had visited and come to know Bill and the Farms simply talked about integrity, quality, friendliness, and the people of Murff's Turf as good, down home folks. As is almost always the case with this type of advertising, it has been extremely well received.

Contrast this approach with so many businesses of today that use sexual innuendo and a thousand other inappropriate and often demeaning approaches to attract people's interest. One case in point was the Calvin Klein advertisements that involved lewd poses by young teenagers that were eventually pulled because of their extreme offensiveness. Thousands of other businesses have used sexually oriented promotions that tend to tear down the morals of society rather than fostering positive values.

And the worst offender of all is the movie industry. I have often thought that the greatest of all missed opportunities in the history of mankind must be the opportunity the great majority of moviemakers have forfeited to shape positive societal values, choosing rather to exploit society's basest, ugliest, and most violent aspects in pursuit of money. They defend themselves by saying they are merely "reflecting society's values." In truth, they are initially reflecting the basest values of a few who would tear the moral fabric of society apart for their own selfish gratification. Tragically, these values begin to permeate the society after years and years of steady exposure and eventually become the norm.

But there will come a time early in the twenty-first century when society will rebel against the destruction of its moral fabric by degrading advertising and exploitation by the movie industry and demand that business, whatever kind, foster positive values. Rejection of this destructive behavior on the part of some businesses has already begun, even being denounced by American presidents and other political leaders.

A society cannot long tolerate moral pollution any more than it can tolerate environmental pollution. Unfortunately, societies seem to come to this realization only after near self-destruction or complete self-destruction. Our society is not too far from these conditions, which will result in Providential purging of society of its evils and the reintroduction of sound moral values. "Righteousness exalteth a nation, but sin is a reproach to any people" (Proverbs 14:34).

There are, at the same time, many notable examples of modern businesses proactively seeking to help shape positive societal values. Most notable for a long time was the Walt Disney Company, which, to a great extent, still fosters positive and family values. But even Walt Disney has wavered in recent years and has chosen to profit from some morally destructive products in order to serve the bottom line rather than the best interests of society.

Business of the twenty-first century must come to finally accept its mission to help shape positive values. The churches cannot do it all. And positive values have long since been stripped out of our schools by amoral judges who have responded to the ACLU and the Madalyn Murray O'Hair's of our society. A few schools have reinstituted values education, however, and where values traditional values have been taught in public schools in recent years, the results have been dramatically positive. It is a certainty that, unless traditional values are regenerated within our society soon, there will not be an orderly society in which to operate a business.

13) Serve Barbecue (or Pizza)

In Texas, barbecue is huge. It is as large as pizza and bagels are in New York City. I grew up eating Texas barbecue, and I never could find any barbecue like Texas barbecue outside of Texas. I always missed it for the thirty-five years I was gone. Texas barbecue is real barbecue, cooked slowly for up to sixteen hours at 220 degrees in a closed pit with a real hardwood fire. All businesses in Texas serve their people barbecue. Barbecue is to Texans like vodka is to Russians. It is the great unifier. It bonds people together. When people have met their goals or done their jobs well in Texas, a barbecue is held. Barbecue, pinto beans, coleslaw, and potato salad are the just rewards of winners in Texas.

When I was at the 1997 Texas Barbecue Cook-Off, I saw hundreds of different kinds of barbecue pits that businesses had built to cook barbecue for their people and their clients. They were in every size and shape, including the largest barbecue pit in the world. Some were on flatbed trucks, some were shaped like steam locomotives, one was in the shape of Texas. The air was thick with the smell of hickory smoke. And hundreds of businesses were treating their customers to the best barbecue in the world.

The day I arrived back in Texas, Bill had served barbecue sandwiches to a group of prison inmates out for the day on a work release program. They each ate three sandwiches; Bill joyfully served up ninety sandwiches the thirty inmates. He still had enough left over to bring my son and me plenty for our supper that first night. And I ate it for several nights following. And he makes sure that his employees get plenty of high-quality barbecue from his pit to assure them of his appreciation for their service.

The point is that food is a way for a business to demonstrate its love for its people. When I was at Mrs. Fields Inc., we always felt Debbie and Randy's love for us with the cookies, muffins, pizzas, and other treats that frequently came from their test ovens. At the time, I had nine children at home, and I will never forget the time that I was given a freezer full of the cookies of many different varieties that Debbie was perfecting. We virtually subsisted on those cookies during a period when we were especially financially challenged.

Pizza and bagels work just as well to reward people for jobs well done. When I was at the State of Utah, pizza was a sure way to attract people to our monthly team days where we would brainstorm ways of improving our service to our clients and our own people. Of course, food has always been a way to get people to show up, and I believe the twenty-first-century business needs to take full advantage of good food to reward its people for work well done.

When I was growing up in Clute, Texas, we lived across the street from a poor family by the name of Goode. They were wonderful people, and John Goode and I were best friends throughout my childhood. John had a younger brother by the name of James. Our circumstances were very adverse in that dirt-poor community of ex-farmers who had come off the farm to work for Dow. I would never have believed that little Jim Goode would have amounted to anything in adulthood. While John and I eventually graduated from Texas

A&M with mechanical engineering degrees, Jim was not academically inclined, nor could his parents afford to send him to college.

But Jim learned how to cook real Texas barbecue. And he is now one of the most successful restaurateurs in Houston. I met Jim some time ago after not having seen him for almost forty years. He was outside of one of his extremely popular Goode Company™ barbecue restaurants cooking barbecue. I asked him why he was doing this. He replied that he was just trying to put some good barbecue smoke flavor into the air to create that sense of homeliness, of country, of down home goodness that people everywhere cherish so much.

In the twenty-first century, the smart business will regularly serve up some good barbecue, pizza, bagels, or whatever it is that turns the people on in their geographical area. The cost of this practice will be more than offset by the loyalty, gratitude, and camaraderie that it will develop.

14) Stay Friendly

One thing that strikes anyone who deals with Murff's Turf Farms is its friendliness. In almost all business transactions, people are looking for friendliness as well as quality products and services. Bill derives more joy from friendships than he ever has from making money. He befriends everyone he sees. Every person he comes into contact with is someone that has something to offer him in the way of wisdom, wit, humor, or just plain friendship.

Not long after I arrived, one of Bill's highly successful landscapers flew down from Dallas to visit and to ride around the fields with him. He and Bill had become good friends over the years and cherished their friendship, periodically visiting each other's operations. The friendship had become more important than their mutually profitable business dealings.

A big part of Bill's workday is "friendshipping" people. He rides around and friendships the harvesters, the maintenance people, the neighbors, the local merchants, and anyone else that he encounters. A good business is a friendly business. A good business is one where you don't sense the drive for revenues but rather the business's interest in you as a person.

I found out the power of the friendliness in my lowly job as Arby's in Orem, Utah. I tried to befriend everyone that came in, and I had some wonderful experiences as I worked the counter every day at noon. Soon I had people coming back for dinner because of the friendship they had experienced at lunch. I had never been able to remember names, but for some reason, at Arby's, I was able to remember regular customers' names. And when they came in, I always tried to make them feel special. I was not making much money, but I was receiving something money could not buy in the return of my customers' friendship toward me. Many of my customers spoke to the manager about how they felt, and one called the company's home office to comment on my treatment of them.

One morning, a woman came in and ordered food for a party for a number of children that were at her home. She paid with a check, and a few minutes after she left, I realized I had left part of the order out. I asked the supervisor if I could leave the store for a few minutes and deliver the food, and he encouraged me to go. Using the address on the check, I found the woman's house just as she was about to serve the food and I cheerfully delivered the rest of the food. Needless to say, she was impressed by our friendliness and service, and I imagine she is a good, loyal customer now.

One of Benjamin Franklin's great secrets as an outstandingly successful businessman was his friendliness. He made friends with almost everyone. When he first became a member of the Pennsylvania Assembly after having served for years as its clerk, he encountered one assemblyman who was jealous and resentful of him and who initially scorned him and spoke disparagingly to others about him. Franklin eventually learned that the man possessed a large library of books, including a rare book he wanted to read. So he approached the assemblyman and asked if he could borrow the book. The man agreed, and upon returning the book, Franklin was profuse in his appreciation. He and the formerly disdainful assemblyman became lifelong friends as a result of this incident.

More than ever, a twenty-first century business will need to be a friendly place to work and to do business with. Every person needs to feel that he or she is important. The chief executives, coaches, facilitators, and team leaders need to take time daily to just walk around and be friends with their people. People will not work long in an unfriendly place of business—or do business with unfriendly people. In the twenty-first century, every business will have to be a friendly business.

15) Simplify

Murff's Turf Farms is remarkable for its simplicity. There are state-of-the-art computers, but payroll, accounting, and other systems are kept as simple as possible. As technology marches on, it is tempting to keep replacing systems with the latest enhancements and keep adding more layers of complexity. Inasmuch as the vendors are in the business of moving hardware and software—and not necessarily in the business of providing solutions for users—it is important to think twice before jumping in on the latest technology craze.

When I arrived at Murff's Turf Farms, I soon realized that they did not have an effective preventive maintenance program for their machinery. Since that was one of my specialties, I quickly identified this need as an area in which I could make a contribution. I had used an inexpensive, wonderfully simple, and user-friendly Windows 3.1 system before. I called the vendor of this software package who convinced me to purchase a Windows 95 version of the program. Upon installing it, however, I was shocked at the inordinate level of complexity it had moved to. Response time had deteriorated markedly, and the user-friendliness had disappeared. I returned the program and reverted to the 3.1 version. The same can be said of people's experience with, for example, Window's Vista. Everyone had to have it, but after acquiring it, found it was too complex and crashed frequently. Many eventually reverted to Windows XP.

In all facets of a business, simplicity should reign as much as possible. A complex business is often not very responsive to its customers and its own people. And the statistics indicate, as I have stated before, that expenditures on office automation simply have not improved bottom-line productivity very much. Office automation has made many tasks infinitely more efficient than before its advent, but work is comprised of processes, which computers do not address. That is why it is important to have people meet often and keep improving the work processes, rather than having the data processing people forever installing more software and hardware to speed up tasks. Once the task has been automated with basic data processing tools, most of the return comes from analyzing the interaction of people in the work processes.

I asked Bill, for example, if he had a strategic plan. He responded that he had never really set long-range goals. I asked if he had a cash-flow management system, and again the answer was no. I asked if had done any formal customer surveys, and again the answer was no. As I went on, it was apparent that he had kept the business very simple. Yet, the farm had steadily grown, stayed in financial control, and prospered over the years. As the complexity of the business had increased, he had delegated more and more of the details to his people, while continuing to do the thing he was best at: friendshipping customers, developing people, and farming. Providence apparently took care of the strategic planning.

On the other hand, at one of my jobs, the founders centralized everything, computerized everything, and held on to all of the power. They continued to involve themselves in the finer details of the business, thinking that, with all the automation, they could know everything and manage everything. Not surprisingly, the company eventually went into decline, and they lost control of it.

It seems as if almost all large companies feel the necessity of having a computerized answering system with a number of options one has to choose from—and oftentimes, several strings of options. While I understand that it becomes impractical to keep adding full-time receptionists to answer ever-increasing volumes of calls, I cannot help but believe there must be some way to maintain the existence of an intelligent human being who answers the phone and directs calls properly. To me, this task would be an ideal one to distribute amongst telecommuters, working from home, with all the tools and training to route calls properly. And, of course, there are answering services that could handle this task well. In any case, when a business has become too complex to have a person answer the phone, it is too complex.

With the bewildering degree of complexity embedded in almost all organizations, it will be increasingly important to focus on simplifying things during the twenty-first century. I believe genuine simplification is still possible. The key to staying as simple as possible is to allow the front-line people, the users of systems, to select the hardware and software rather than letting the financial people and the data processing people select them. Invariably, if the latter condition is allowed to prevail, systems will be far too complex and almost always designed to serve the accountants' purposes rather than the people who interact with customers and do the operational and administrative functions of the business.

The goal of the data processing people and the accountants is almost invariably to achieve massive integration of the database. But there is a level at which too much integration becomes counterproductive, and the goal of everyone knowing everything is not realistic.

There is still a place for standalone systems designed to do exactly what the operators want them to do with no regard for the purported needs of the accountants and the managers. Whatever the case, people who run businesses need to keep in mind that the goal is to develop people and to serve customers—with as little complexity as possible. Otherwise, in the twenty-first century, the electronic tail will be wagging the organizational dog to a degree that will be destructive to the business.

16) Spend Time with Vendors

In more than one office, I have seen a poster that has a six-shooter staring you in the face with a stern cowboy saying, "We shoot every third salesman that comes in here. The second one just left." In fact, many organizations get to the point where they put a sign on the front door that says "No Soliciting." I have come to believe that that is a mistake; vendors are a wonderful source of information on competitors and on state-of-the-art developments in the field.

Rather than seeing solicitors as nuisances and time-wasters, I have always welcomed a break in my day during which I could pick a salesperson's brains about everything under the sun pertaining to his product and his product users. I always learned much from them, and even when they did not make a sale, they have become better salespeople by visiting me. And, usually, I have made a friend whose product I will eventually need in my business. When a business or a businessperson gets to the point of rejecting all salespeople except the one he or she seeks out, I believe they have become too insular to remain on the cutting edge of their field.

An experience I had at Murff's Turf Farms serves to bear this belief out for me. A salesman for Bucyrus Equipment's Magnum 42 harvester visited us and demonstrated his equipment. It was a cold February day, and we braved a biting east wind for several hours while he demonstrated his harvester. The salesman had just come from Florida and had previously been all over the country visiting with sod farmers. He was knowledgeable about harvesting practices of every kind, and we picked his brain incessantly. We came to genuinely like this salesman, brought him home for barbecue, and learned more than we could have possibly expected to from him.

Because he had the Cadillac of the industry in harvesters, which cost a great deal more money than Murff's Turf was interested in spending, we knew in the beginning that we would not buy his machine. Still, his visit was highly beneficial. Bill, of course, was thinking of how he might maximize the value of this visit and create some kind of business synergy. His mind soon turned to one of his former agriculture students that he had helped launch in the grass business. This individual had perfected Bill's St. Augustine sprig spreader and had built Bill's beautiful, high-quality home without blueprints. Bill considered him a genius.

Steve had decided that he would build his own harvester from scratch, and he was confident he could build a better one than the ones on the market. As with Bill's house, he didn't bother to draw any plans or formalize a design; he simply bought a load of metal and started welding. Five months and $24,000 later, he had a revolutionary new harvester design in full working order. Bill was so impressed with it that he was constantly urging him to market it commercially and arranged for the Bucyrus salesman to look at Steve's new harvester design with a view toward getting Bucyrus to market it.

I don't know whether anything will ever come of this interaction, but everyone benefited and learned a great deal from all of the discussions and demonstrations that went on during that morning. And we made a good friend in the process.

With the proliferation of telemarketing and an every-increasing number of sales calls, the tendency will be to become more defensive toward vendor salespeople. But in the twenty-first century, the people who remain open to sales calls and learn to see salespeople as valuable resources will be the winners.

When I went to time management training many years ago with one of the pioneers in that business, part of his program was teaching the attendees how to subtly get salespeople and other interrupters out of their offices quickly. The idea was that you should spend time with no one that was not on your list of "A" priorities—and then only use the minimum possible time to meet your goal and earn a checkmark for that item on your daily to-do list. For several years, I tried to get this individual to meet with me to discuss some of my business concepts. I never did get an appointment with him. His business eventually went into decline and no longer exists; I cannot help but believe his insularity helped put him out of business.

Business is about people, and since I have had an opportunity to observe hundreds of Bill's interactions with people, I have become more convinced than ever that everyone we encounter has a precious gem of wisdom, a gift to give us, and we them. It will be our job in the coming century to perfect the art of making the most of every interaction and to mine the treasures of knowledge that vendors have acquired from their contacts with scores of businesses like ours. I believe the good will and networks that will derive from this practice will more than compensate us for the time spent.

17) Share the Gains

Bill employs about forty field laborers. While it is fairly common for businesses to share gains in one form or another, I had never heard of field laborers enjoying this benefit. Bill shares the profits with all of his people, including the field laborers. He has also built homes for his foremen and provides free housing for them. Not surprisingly, he attracts the brightest and the best people in the area—and they become tremendously loyal and productive. His lead foreman has been with him for almost thirty years.

Profit sharing is a no-brainer for business leaders and must be a vital part of the globally competitive twenty-first-century business. Coupled with employee ownership through stock purchase plans, this practice—when implemented with the economic utility principles discussed in chapter 4—elicits people's deepest commitment and highest motivation to excel at their jobs. Corporate performance is maximized when ownership and appropriate profit-sharing approaches are utilized.

Bill has deeded much of his farm to his children. Even in a family business, ownership is vital. All of his children have become wealthy in the business with the commitment and hard work elicited by profit sharing and ownership in the business.

18) Start Paying a Fair Wage

A fair wage for a person is a wage that is directly proportionate to that person's contribution to the business. Bill's lead handyman earns $60,000 a year. That is an unheard of wage for a handyman. But this man saves Bill a hundred thousand dollars a year in avoided service calls on the equipment, on avoided contractor costs for new buildings, and on many other avoided costs. He can fix anything. He doesn't need direction. He just comes to work every morning and does whatever needs to done to make the equipment run and the farm work. He has been with Bill for twenty-nine years and, because he is fairly compensated, there is no danger of him leaving.

When I went to work for Macys and Arby's, both of them asked me what I needed as a wage. I asked for significantly more than what the going rate was, and both of them paid me what I asked. They recognized that I would bring to the business more than a teenager would. They wanted to pay me fairly, and I believe I exceeded their expectations.

Before I went to work for the State of Utah, my soon-to-be supervisor asked what I needed for a salary. I told him, and he made a counteroffer of significantly more than I had asked for. He knew that, with my background, I would be able to more than earn the liberal salary that he had proposed. And he continued to raise my salary year after year and upgrade me until I was probably the best paid staffer in the state. I gave him far more than he paid for. I was hired to install a preventive maintenance program in state-owned facilities, and I went far beyond that, leading the division to a comprehensive Total Quality Management strategy.

But in a large corporate environment, it is always difficult to determine a fair wage for each employee. The result is that employees in similar positions, as determined by the human resources department, are paid similar salaries regardless of the degree of their actual contribution to the business. I believe there are two ways wage fairness can be improved in the corporate environment.

One way to improve wage fairness is for a company to offer a competitive wage and to also share profits. Invariably, such a philosophy attracts the brightest and best people to the company, which renders it highly competitive and capable of attracting the brightest and best in its field. The instability and continual turnover that low wages cause always end up costing companies far more than the marginal costs of wage leadership. With the turnover resulting from low wages, there is the cost of constantly training new people, of low quality during the learning curve, of poor response time to customers, and all of the other side effects of dissatisfied people.

I offer another way to help bring about wage equity in chapter 13. I believe that with proper self-measurement of performance, any knowledge worker's actual contribution to revenues can be determined. This proposed approach is a radical change from today's often inequitable approaches. In the twenty-first century, wages will have to be based on a person's actual contributions to the revenues of the business.

But often, a fair wage and a living wage are not the same. A competitive or leading edge wage in the twenty-first century may still not be a living wage. With more competition and customers demanding greater value, prices will have to be so low that it will be difficult to pay a living wage. This condition will almost demand that gainsharing approaches be utilized. Gainsharing is a win-win way to provide adequate compensation in a highly competitive environment.

Many companies are successfully using gainsharing as a way to allow people to earn more while making the business more competitive. Nucor Steel has always allowed its people to, as teams, identify ways to cut costs and increase revenues and to share the gains from these improvements. And it has long been one of the lowest-cost producers with some of the highest-paid steel workers in the industry.

Some years ago, American Express decided to implement a gainsharing program in its West Valley, Utah, credit card center. They simply made the decision to do it, formed a cross-functional team to work out the details, and had the program implemented within three months. It has brought about significantly improved service, lower costs of doing business, and has allowed people to earn significant bonuses.

At Murff's Turf Farms, I was surprised to learn that everyone received bonuses based on the number of yards of grass sold. Of course, most of the people had nothing to do with the selling of the grass, but knowing that they will profit from the farm's success has made everyone more conscientious so that more grass is available to sell. Bill finds many ways to compensate people. He has built a nice home on the property for his lead hourly worker. He serves lunch daily for his office people. He provides daycare for his office workers.

The twenty-first-century business will have to come to see people as the purpose of the business and to find ways to compensate them on the basis of their actual contributions to the bottom line. And gainsharing will have to become a way of life in the twenty-first century.

19) Stick with Teams

In the United States, a lot of organizations have given up on making teams work. After failing to find reasons to continue to meet, everyone has retreated to the safety of their computers, where they sit for forty hours per week, shielded from formal interaction with other members of their work group. This condition is unfortunate and terribly wasteful of human potential. It denies the organization the incredible synergy that is possible when people become highly performing teams.

Certainly, the problem with teams in the United States is not that Americans do not enjoy teamwork. Interest in team sports in the United States, for example, has almost risen to the level of religion. And during World War II, the entire country became a totally unified, highly synergistic team dedicated to the singular purpose of winning the war. Teams of every size and type were formed in hundreds of realms that achieved almost impossible tasks in unthinkably short time spans.

But in times other than a crisis, it is difficult in a highly individualistic society to make genuine teamwork a permanent part of the organizational culture. A lack of understanding of cultural norms governs the thinking about teamwork in the United States. In chapter 4, I discuss this phenomenon in detail and suggest ways to embed teamwork into the organizational culture.

When I arrived at Murff's Turf Farms, teamwork was deeply embedded in the organization. Geographically, the farm was arranged so that interaction and integration of the various functions of the farm was natural and inevitable. The trucks were parked on the property when they were not in, although owned by someone else. The trucker lived next door to the farm. The shops were close to the administrative offices.

Every morning a team meeting was conducted to synchronize the operation. Locations of cutting operations, mowing, fertilizing, and other tasks were synergistically arrived at in a very short period of time. Further interaction of the administration people occurred every day at the team luncheon. Everyone had radios and constantly communicated with each other. Like a hive of bees, it was filled with harmonious activity and almost devoid of central control.

I quickly initiated weekly team meetings using formal problem-solving tools. For the first time, I brought some of the mechanics and other front-line people into the formal continuous improvement process. I conducted only one of these meetings. Because people must experience personal growth in order to maintain interest in formal problem-solving meetings, it was my intent to quickly involve every member of the team in the conduct of the meetings.

American workers must have a personal stake in the teamwork process. They must feel that teamwork is not as much for solving organizational problems as for their own growth and development. Once people experience this growth taking place, it becomes an important part of their agenda. It is this lure that gets people involved, but once involved, something else takes place if the team's goal is clearly enough defined and lofty enough. People eventually experience the feeling of synergy that athletic teams experience, the thrill of jointly achieving excellence, the joy of striving together with others in a worthy cause.

It is important for the twenty-first-century business to not give up on teams. The more inherently group-oriented societies of the Pacific Rim have perfected the art of teamwork and have consequently led a manufacturing quality and productivity revolution. If the United States is to compete in the global economy, our organizations must not give up on teams as we enter the twenty-first century.

20) Symbolize Rural Values

Before W. Edwards Deming died, I had the opportunity to attend one of his seminars at the Utah State University Partners Program. As he went through his fourteen points for management, it struck me that the traditional American farm adhered to every one of his points and avoided every one of his seven deadly sins.

I asked Mr. Deming if he thought that was why the American farmer had no equals in productiveness in the world. By the time I succeeded in getting him to hear what I was asking, I was thoroughly embarrassed in front of a crowd of hundreds of executives. But he finally did concur with me.

After more than twenty years of studying business, it should not have been surprising to me that my research would finally lead me to the farm. It was only there that I was able to summarize my quest in the form of twenty-two (five more were added later) ground rules for the twenty-first-century business.

Farming is one of the very few businesses in America that has not been threatened with dominance by offshore competitors. Of course, part of the reason for the success of agriculture in America is topographical and climatic. We simply have more and better land and climates than most other farmers in the world. But there is much more to the story of the success of America's farms than that.

There is something inherently good about the independent farmer in America. There is a sense of family, a unity of purpose, a common goal of survival. There is sufficient amount of solitude during which a man and a woman and children can hear the still small voice that resides within each of us. The farm is morally purifying. There is exposure to the beauties of nature, the constant observation of the reproduction and nurturing of life. There is the absolute necessity of teamwork.

There is not the pursuit of short-term profits at the expense of the future of the organization. There has to be a long-term perspective in farming. There is the most concentric of organization structure. There is friendliness with the neighbors and the willingness always to lend a hand. There is the idea that life is about family, the pursuit of liberty and happiness, and that happiness in rooted in virtues, hard work, and a partnership with God.

Unfortunately, with the move from an agrarian to an industrial and now to an information economy, we have, along the way, lost some of that connectedness to the soil and some of the values that made America great, and our country is suffering from that loss.

It occurred to me that I, too, had moved from an agrarian beginning on a remote black land farm, to an industrial career as a power engineer, from there to a computerized information systems administrator, and had now, finally returned to the soil. I had lost some of the great values of my youth, and it had cost me dearly. But having lost everything, I had turned back to that God who had given me breath and, with my feet back on the ground, I had hope that maybe I could rebuild my life.

As the small farm becomes more and more a thing of our past, we would do well to continue to study the farm and how it formed the foundation for the greatness of America. As we move into the twenty-first century with our heads in the clouds, we need to keep our feet firmly planted on the ground.

21] Set a Goal and Accept a Mission

In appendix 3, I issue challenges to both American business leaders and to the great American white-collar workforce. For the leaders, the challenge is to accept the mission to *develop the full potential of your people.* This task will require your full commitment and will bring far more joy and satisfaction than downsizing an acquired company ever could. It will be the greatest challenge of your career and will be the greatest service you could ever hope to render to your country.

To workers, your challenge is to follow the example of the most productive mortal to ever live, Benjamin Franklin, and the admonition of the CEO of this galaxy, Jesus Christ, and to pursue *moral perfection.* While you will not achieve the goal in this life, the character developed in the effort will open the wellsprings of achievement, and you will no doubt become the most productive people in the history of work.

The single, superordinate, unifying goal I am challenging both leaders and the workforce to set is to *restore America's founding values.* Since the sexual revolution and the accelerated secularization of our society that began in the 1960s, America's reputation as a virtuous nation has rapidly declined with its abandonment of its founding values, while it has chosen instead, materialism, hedonism, and merger mania with its inexorable downsizing and exportation of U.S. jobs. This restoration is possible with the recommitment to our founding documents, the concept of developmentship introduced in this book, and the moral leadership of our national and business leaders.

The power of a sense of singular mission and a national superordinate goal cannot be overestimated. Without such, our country is truly floundering, and the moral fabric of our country is coming apart. We cannot long survive as a nation when we are losing so much of our precious human capital to the abyss of selfish dissipation.

When our liberty was threatened during World War II, we united with a common mission to subdue multiple tyrants' quests for world domination. Our country, with a singular purpose, went from a deep economic depression to the mightiest military-industrial complex the world has ever known in a matter of a very short time.

Today, the enemies of freedom are just as real but much more subtle than were the tyrants of the 1930s and '40s. One of these enemies is a lack of vision and purpose. Solomon said, "Where there is no vision, the people perish" (Proverbs 29:18). And now, for the past hundred or more years, we have been continuously subjected to the false idea that man is a product of evolution, that he is an animal, that there is consequently no moral code, and there is no eternal purpose for mankind.

The fact is that mankind is the offspring of God. God is the invisible hand in our economy. He is the author of democracy and the source of free enterprise. All of the creation bears witness of this reality. His work and his glory is that of bringing about the immortality and eternal life of man. He is interested in the development of each person's unique gifts and the preservation of the family unit.

That is why the mission of the enterprise and the twenty-first-century business leader must be to see work as a means to develop people, rather than seeing people as a means to get work done. That is why management must be replaced by *developmentship* in the twenty-first century. That is why the goal must be to reestablish America's reputation for goodness. Only then will we be able to revolutionize quality and productivity. Only by a return to our founding values can we remain a free nation.

22) Sow Seeds in All Available Soil

While I was nearing completion of this manuscript, my eighty-five-year-old father died. He was another great man of the soil. At the funeral, the minister dwelt upon his legendary love of the soil and how he planted every available plot of ground in something. He told of the time he went to my father's place only to find peas planted and growing right in the middle of the long drive leading up to the house. The peas had been trained by the passing of cars over them and were growing sideways and flourishing.

That story reminded me of the St. Augustine sod Bill was growing under the power company's high voltage transmission lines. The power company welcomed this intrusion, because it meant that they needed to do no maintenance on this mile or two of right of way. It always stayed beautifully mowed and planted. Bill called this field the Highline Field, and it had generated significant revenues.

During my career of building and operating power plants, I was always amazed by how much capital was invested and how much of its potential was not being realized. I took a position as a plant manager of a new coal-fired power plant that was to be built on three thousand acres of land, only a relatively few which was to be occupied by the plant and its ancillaries. Having considerable time on my hands during the dirt-moving phase of construction, I gave a lot of thought into how to put the rest of the land to use and suggested a number of uses to the company's management. They demonstrated no interest, even though their projected power rates as a result of the massive investment in the plant were projected to rise dramatically, and additional sources of revenue could have helped offset some of this rise.

One power plant at which I worked sought to literally plant seeds in all available soil. This plant was under environmental regulations that required zero discharge of water from the plant. So the company developed a large farm on the land it owned surrounding the plant, and used the wastewater from the plant to irrigate the farm. They also sold ash to a company that made concrete, sulfur dioxide from the stack scrubbers, and generated revenue from the sale of coal, and any other way they could. As a consequence, their rate increases resulting from new plant construction were relatively moderate.

I believe that return on investment is still one the best measures of a company's performance and that every effort will have to be made in the coming century to maximize this return on capital. Bill has carefully sold off much of the frontage property on his farm and replaced it with other property in order to maximize his return on land investment. His is subdividing the wooded property, has a reservoir leased to a hunting company, acreage leased to a large radio-controlled airplane association, and appears to be maximizing the return on his land investments.

My forty-year career in business convinced me that most businesses have a great deal of fallow soil, both intellectual and otherwise. But during the twenty-first century, I believe it will be necessary to sow seeds in all available soil in order to stay competitive.

Five Additional Essentials

Since my four-month sojourn on Murff's Turf farm in 1996, the ever-evolving business environment has brought several other essentials for the twenty-first-century business to light, as follows:

23) Sell on the Social Networks

Social media has become an essential platform for business marketing strategy in the twenty-first century. More than 65 million Americans are now regularly accessing social media sites. This new phenomenon has dramatically increased communication for organizations and fosters brand awareness and, often, improved customer service. Additionally, social media serves as a relatively inexpensive platform for organizations to implement marketing campaigns. With emergence of Twitter, FaceBook, YouTube, and blogs, personalized and niche marketing opportunities for businesses have been significantly expanded.

Social media marketing programs center on efforts to create content that attracts attention and encourages readers to share it with their social networks. A corporate message spreads from user to user and resonates because it is coming from a trusted, third-party source, as opposed to the brand or company itself.

Cell phone usage has also become an important benefit for social media marketing. Today, many cell phones have social networking capabilities; individuals are notified of any happenings on social networking sites through their cell phones—in real-time. This constant connection to social networking sites means products and companies can continually remind and update followers about their capabilities, uses, importance, etc. Because cell phones are connected to social networking sites, advertisements are always in sight.

In summary, SMO (social media optimization), like the dot.com revolution of the '90s can no longer be ignored by marketers of the twenty-first century business. It must become an integral part of a cutting-edge marketing strategy and a strategy for maximizing business performance.

24) Stem Medical Benefit Costs with Prevention

Approximately 75 percent of today's healthcare costs stem from preventable chronic diseases like heart disease, Type 2 diabetes, and some forms of cancer. What's more, the productivity impact of these conditions is significant for organizations. The lost economic output associated with chronic conditions totals more than $1 trillion, including time lost for employee and caregiver workdays and individual and caregiver absenteeism.

Forward-looking businesses are taking action to lower healthcare costs by implementing programs that help employees make healthier lifestyle choices. These companies understand the significant medical and productivity cost impact of an unhealthy workforce and recognize the vital role they play in encouraging their employees to be healthy. Studies prove the workplace is an ideal environment for fostering good health. They provide powerful social networks to keep employees engaged and motivated in good health. Effectively structured and implemented incentives-based wellness programs drive down healthcare costs by keeping people healthy and preventing the onset of chronic conditions. Leading businesses know they must create a workplace culture of health to avoid a profitability crisis of epic proportions.

Studies show an average 27 percent reduction in sick leave when a company adds a wellness program and a 26 percent reduction in health-care costs. Wellness programs have also been shown to reduce employee turnover and even to lure employees to a company.

So, wellness programs must become an essential facet of the twenty-first-century maximized business.

25) Stimulate Innovation by Emulating Google

Much can be learned from Google in seeking to maximize business performance. Started in a garage in Menlo Park, California, in 1998, Google has grown into a world-changing organization with a market value of close to two hundred billion dollars. Its stock price is consistently one of the highest on the market. It is one of the most innovative companies in the world, and the reason is no secret.

Google attracts the best and brightest people with its *developmentship* corporate culture. Its employees are encouraged to spend 20 percent of their time on personal pet projects. A tremendous amount of innovation comes out of this liberating and potential-maximizing philosophy. Maximizing business performance in the twenty-first century will require companies to find ways to tap into the enormous reservoir of hidden potential within their intellectual capital. Tapping this potential is one of the primary objectives of the *developmentship* philosophy.

Google has clearly defined and strives to constantly implement its three highest values. Not surprisingly, they are all people-oriented. *We work with the best people in the world. Working at Google is fun. Innovative technology drives our success.*

Here are ten reasons identified by Avinash Kaushik after a year at Google that have enabled Google to able to maximize its performance: "... fantastic food and impressive digs; a company that truly cares; brain expansion opportunities; the sheer amount of brilliant Google employees; empowerment (the big small company); the scale of your impact; doing good; green technology; it's a happening place; the energy, the vibe, the passion, the brand."

Here is how Kaushik and many others describe working at Google: "Interesting, fun, surprising, insightful, inspiring, impactful." Of course, not all of Google's approaches are appropriate at every business. But the business that is genuinely interested in maximizing its performance can surely find much at Google to emulate, and the Google workplace culture should be studied and emulated in its fundamental understanding of human performance by every business that seeks to maximize its performance.

26) Save on Energy Costs with Green Technologies

With ever-increasing energy costs and increasingly stringent environmental constraints, the use of green technologies can no longer be ignored by businesses of any size. America's past disregard of energy conservation has provided most businesses with many opportunities to cut operating costs and reduce the environmental impact of their operations.

Studies have shown over a twenty-year period, some green buildings have yielded $53 to $71 per square foot back on investment.

Confirming the rentability of green building investments, further studies of the commercial real estate market have found that LEED- and Energy Star-certified buildings achieve significantly higher rents, sale prices, and occupancy rates as well as lower capitalization rates, potentially reflecting lower investment risk.

Of course, there are almost limitless opportunities for cutting energy costs, even in preexisting facilities. And in many cases, there are various kinds of financial incentives for energy conservation available from power companies, government agencies, and suppliers. Every company should mount an employee-driven energy-conservation program. Motivated by various kinds of incentives, employees can find scores of ways to cut waste in the use of natural resources and energy in their workplaces.

Without question, conservation and environmental friendliness are essentials for the twenty-first-century business.

27) Standardize Financial Reporting

XBRL (eXtensible Business Reporting Language) is a relatively new, standardized electronic format for reporting business financial information. SEC filings of over $5 billion began to be required in this new format in 2009, and the scope of the SEC filing mandate will be gradually expanded. But even though the use of XBRL is not expected be become a general financial reporting mandate, businesses can benefit significantly by moving to a standardized financial reporting system. For too long, business financial statements and accounting data have had diverse and often incomprehensible semantics. Such fuzzy reporting has resulted in not a few businesses being found guilty of filing fraudulent financial reports that skew profit-and-loss data.

It is therefore essential that the twenty-first-century business moves toward adopting the XBRL standards of financial reporting.

Over my more than fifty years in business, I have always been struck by the contrast between the core values of agricultural operations and those of industrial operations. I first noticed this stark contrast at Texas A&M University. At the time, Texas A&M was an all-male military school; everyone lived together in dormitories. Admittedly not a business environment, it was nonetheless a unique opportunity to see the remarkable difference in the values learned on farms and ranches and those brought from the large urban environments by the generally more affluent and amoral students from the big cities such as Dallas and Houston. The "country boys" almost universally had better study habits and higher moral values than those from the big cities.

Conclusion

Bill Murff epitomizes the foundational leadership and developmentship paradigms better than anyone I have ever worked with or studied. The twenty-first-century business leader can learn much from his life.

CHAPTER 12
Maximizing Personal Freedom

This book has been about freedom at work. It has introduced new organizational science that can maximize freedom and performance in the knowledge work environment. And because the 21st century workplace is orders of magnitude more competitive than that of the last century when America dominated the world's economies, it is now essential for U.S. workers to move to an entirely new plateau of performance. Anything less will assuredly result in further expropriation of American jobs by offshore competitors.

Moving to this new plateau of performance, together with government policies more favorable to U.S. business and the return of America to its constitutional principles, can lead once again to career security and the restoration of a rising trend in our national standard of living. It will not, however, necessarily result in a maximization of individual happiness and personal freedom. Maximizing personal freedom and the joy that derives from it requires not only a new plateau of performance in the workplace, but just as importantly, building the other facets of one's life on the universal principles of life success. The growing secularization, immorality, and materialism that is eating away at America's founding values and destroying the traditional family in America will not lead to individual happiness regardless of how high performing one is in the workplace.

Values brought to America by the Puritans, inculcated into the moral fabric of the country by teachings from the pulpit and from the Bible in America's homes and schools, by publications like Benj. Franklin's *Poor Richard's Almanac,* and a once godly press, constituted founding values that made America the best hope of the world for achieving happiness and fulfillment. These values formed the basis of what became known as The American Dream. And while this dream has now become defined almost exclusively as the achievement of material security, affluence, and the liberty to freely utilize these instruments for earthly comfort, recreation, and gratification, this country was raised up by Providence for a higher purpose. That purpose was for America to be a beacon of virtue, a place for the restoration of pure religion, a base for the spread of the Gospel of Jesus Christ throughout the world so that we of the human kind could prepare for our next phase of progress following our brief mortal sojourn.

Notwithstanding the purposes of God for America, His material blessings upon the nation are not predicated upon the adherence of its populace to the Christian or Jewish religions or to a particular church at all. They are, however, without question, directly proportional to the degree of adherence of a majority of the nation's populace to the Ten Commandments and to basic principles of human decency and moral conduct. Statistics on the moral behavior of our population abundantly reveal that America is now at a tipping point in this regard, a point at which a majority of our population has abandoned many of our founding values and moral principles. And, not surprisingly, the nation has begun to experience the inevitable judgments of God upon a people, when a majority of them have abandoned divinely revealed moral standards of conduct. These judgments are not only in the form of increasingly frequent and destructive natural phenomena, but in the rise in unemployment and the decline in a people's standard of living as well.

Because of the absolute prerequisite of national virtue in securing and assuring the continuance of the blessings of Providence upon our nation, God raised up men of towering morality, courage, and commitment to Judeo-Christian values to shape a revolutionary new system of government upon which to build a nation of liberty and virtue. We call these men our founding fathers. There were two halves of the inspired system of government they brought forth, one half of which was recorded upon parchments in the form of The *Mayflower Compact,* the *Declaration of Independence,* and the *Constitution of the United States.* The other half was chiseled in the granite of our national monuments and recorded upon canvas upon the walls of our capitol building. For example, there are no fewer than fifty representations of The Ten Commandments upon and within in our Supreme Court building. When one enters the U.S. Capitol building, he or she is greeted with giant canvases depicting Washington kneeling in prayer, Pocahontas being baptized, of our founders holding the Holy bible, as well as many other depictions of our Judeo-Christian heritage.

One of these great men that God raised up was Benj. Franklin. To no small degree, the original formula (thoroughly documented in his autobiography) for maximizing personal achievement, virtue, and life success sprang from this towering, legendary figure. Likewise, the blueprint for what I call 'foundatioinal leadership' was shaped by the man known as the 'father of our country', George Washington (his legacy is addressed in chapter 7 of this work). Benj. Franklin, like Washington, recognized the absolute necessity of virtue in both achieving personal success and happiness and in building and preserving a prosperous new nation. While he was not particularly enamored with organized religion, he knew there was a God in heaven, from whom all blessings flowed. Benj. Franklin deliberately set out to crystalize thousands of years of divinely revealed truth and the collective wisdom of humankind, in its quest for freedom and happiness since the beginning of recorded history.

In his monumental effort to create a practical collection of the principles of success and virtue, he searched all of the great authorities of history in the field of human performance. He studied the Bible, the writings of Locke, Hume, Montesquieu, Rousseau, Pythagoras, Bacon, Milton, Mather, Plutarch, Defoe, and many others. With this foundation, he sailed to England, and there he crystallized his vision to become all that he was capable of becoming to the benefit his fellow beings and in the development of the free and prosperous new nation of America. His journey followed an only recently fully understood process. That process defined for first time, a maximizing strategy for personal life success. And not surprisingly, Benj. Franklin wrote the first so-called 'success' book, entitled, *The Way to Wealth*. Coupling this strategy with the late Stephen Covey's model for achieving high personal effectiveness and the new organizational science introduced in this work, there is now a comprehensive and holistic route to maximizing one's career potential, personal freedom, and life fulfillment.

Having now succinctly articulated his thirteen universal success principles, Benj. Franklin set out upon the *'bold and arduous project'* of *'achieving moral perfection'*. He determined that he would henceforth strive to adhere to the highest standards of moral conduct and relations with his fellow beings. He soon found, however, that as he focused on achieving perfection in one principle, often a transgression would sneak up on him in one of the others and that it was unrealistic to expect to achieve a high degree of perfection all at once.

Taking a page from Pythagoras' *Little Verses,* he created the first daily self-examination and real-time feedback on performance system for the systematic development of character. He would select one of the 'virtues' and seek to achieve perfection in it for a week, while tracking his failures in the other twelve areas. Each week he would select another area to focus upon and would then try to keep two areas without transgressions. He would thereby in thirteen week cycles, address improvement in each area, gradually achieving a high degree of congruence with his universal principles and values and the 'habitude' of virtue.

Using his system for developing congruence with these universal principles, Benj. Franklin proceeded to become, arguably, the most productive mortal to ever walk the face of the earth. He made major contributions to almost every field of human endeavor and arguably had the most influence of all of the foundering fathers, with the exception of George Washington, in bringing forth the most prosperous and progressive nation in all of human history.

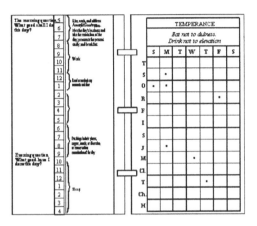

Benj. Franklin's Daily Planner and Real-Time Feedback System

Franklin found that achieving 'order' was the most difficult habit for him to acquire in all of the thirteen virtues. So, he designed his famous and now widely used time-management format. Putting his planner format and his real-time feedback on character development together with red lines on ivory plates that could be erased and reused, Franklin created his 'little book', to which in his latter life he credited with a large measure of his phenomenal success in life.

Benj. Franklin is the ultimate role model for maximizing personal achievement. While the time management half of his success system was restored in the 1940s and since has been widely marketed by a number of companies, only recently has his real-time measurement and feedback system for achieving congruence with universal principles become available as smart phone and tablet computer applications.

To gain insight into the importance and modern day relevance of Franklin's achievement maximizing system, it will be helpful to review the history and development of, and the amazing results that Benj. Franklin attributed to his methodology.

Not long after arriving in Philadelphia, Benj. Franklin, already a skilled printer, working with one, Samuel Keimer, caught the attention of colonial governor William Keith. Keith arranged a meeting with Franklin and was so impressed with the young printer that he suggested the Benj. travel to England, purchase printing equipment, and return to establish his own printing business. He indicated that he would provide letters of credit for the purchases and passage to and from England. These letters were to be given to the ship's captain, to be transferred to Benj. during the voyage. However, upon approaching the captain soon after the ship's departure, Benj. discovered that there were no such letters of credit. He was forced into hard labor during the voyage to pay for passage and arrived in England in a state of destitution.

Being a highly industrious young man, Benj. soon found work with a London printing establishment and quickly made his mark as a highly skilled and productive worker. Having a love of books and culture and now being somewhat prosperous, Franklin fell in love with London and soon determined to make it his permanent residence. After sometime, however, a vision began to form in Benj.'s mind of the great opportunities that he had left behind in the fledging new nation of America. This vision began to grow in intensity, until after a few months, Benj. determined to return to America, marry Deborah Ried, whom he had met upon his initial arrival in Philadelphia, and spend the rest of his life building this new nation.

Within two years after returning to Philadelphia and marrying Deborah Ried, Franklin formed a partnership with one, Hugh Meredith, borrowed capital, and started his own printing business. Because of his skill, work ethic, and commitment, the business soon became the leading printing establishment in Philadelphia. He then established printing ventures in a number of other colonies and even in the Virgin Islands. With his scholarship, skill, and solvency, he, at the age of twenty-five, determined to maximize his service by tapping the wellsprings of human potential, namely, virtue and personal integrity. He set out upon the 'bold and arduous project' of achieving moral perfection'. He developed his now famous day planner for both time management and the systematic development of the 'habitude of virtue'. Achieving amazing harmony with his thirteen 'virtues' and personal values, he seems to have seized every opportunity for service. He totally committed himself to becoming the role model for all time for the self-made man, the super-achiever. And no one has yet been able to fully plumb the depths of his achievements and contributions, although many have tried.

He was motivated by the desire to develop his full potential for service, and not just a desire to achieve financial independence and affluence. By the young age of forty-two, he had a substantial stream of income from his printing ventures and the revenue generated by the widely distributed and best selling, Poor Richard's Almanac. He then promptly retired, turning his business over to his wife, Deborah and trusted associate, David Hall. This decision allowed him to move to the phase of life success called by the famous twentieth century psychologist, Abraham Maslow, *self-actualization*. Self-actualization is the discovery, development, and giving of one's special gift, one's unique ability to bless mankind with something that one can do better than anyone has ever done it before and possibly something that has never been done before. Every one has one or more of these gifts. Benj. Franklin had many, and he systematically developed each one of them to the fullest extent. His work revolutionized life, first in Philadelphia, then in the Colonies, and eventually, in the United States and the world.

One of Franklin's special gifts was his propensity for rigorous analysis of natural phenomena. And at the time, one of the most curious, even fearful natural phenomenons for most people was lightning. In his famous kite and static electricity experiments, Franklin defined the nature of lighting and wrote the first book on electricity. He literally layed the foundation for the modern-day electronic revolution, and in doing so, became world famous, soon being awarded the Copley Gold Metal by the Royal Society of London.

With his fame and financial independence, Franklin was now able to develop and give perhaps his most important gifts of all, that of statesmanship and diplomacy. Having diligently nurtured these skills with his system, his 'little book', during the first half of his life, Franklin spent almost the entire last half of his life in foreign diplomatic service. During his last ten years in England he brilliantly helped facilitate the birth of a wonderful new nation. He then came home and played an indispensible role at the advanced age of eighty-two, in the framing of the Constitution of the United States.

So, this chapter is about a comprehensive life success strategy. The foundation of the system is Franklin's thirteen universal success principles and his system for developing the habits of success in accordance with these principles and values. Complementing Franklin's seminal approach to developing these habits is the more recent work of the late and highly respected Stephen Covey (alluded to above) with his extensively disseminated and well received *7 Habits of Highly Successful People*. Accordingly, some of Covey's important work on developing the habits of success is included in this discussion of maximizing personal freedom.

In developing the 'habitude of virtue' Franklin pioneered real-time, graphical feedback on performance. Since all work is a process, and since no process is in control without real-time feedback, one cannot expect to achieve his or her full potential without real-time measurement and feedback, both in the workplace and in one's life success process. Let us illustrate Benj. Franklin's holistic approach to maximizing personal performance and freedom.

Franklin's Performance
Maximizing Process

Systematically Develop
Habits of Succes

Plan/Checkoff
Daily/Weekly Schedule
& Do List

Daily Prayer
Thnksgiving&Guidance

Personal Mission
Maximize Service

Own   Clarify
Universl Principles/Personal Values

At the base of this metaphorical liberty bell are the thirteen principles of success Franklin identified, and his personal values linked to these principles. Next, up on the bell is Personal Mission. In Franklin's case it was simply to maximize his service to his fellow beings. Stephen Covey was very strong on personal mission, indicating that to him, step one in seeking to become highly successful is using a series of questions about one's life preferences and inner most desires to serve his or her fellow beings, to formulate a succinct personal mission statement indicating how one plans to do this.

Next up on our liberty bell is Daily Prayer. Although Benj. Franklin was not a regular churchgoer, he was a strong believer in the hand of God in the affairs of man and that all blessings flowed from His presence. So, the first thing he did upon rising in the morning was to address Providence in prayer. Here is one of those prayers: "O powerful goodness! Bountiful Father! Merciful Guide! Increase in me that wisdom which discovers my truest interest. Straighten my resolution to perform what that wisdom dictates. Accept my kind offices to thy other children as the only return in my power for thy continued favors to me." It behooves every person who desires to maximize their performance, to kneel before their God, in the morning to seek divine guidance, and in the evening to give thanks for the blessings of the day. "

After prayer, Benj. Would plan his day using the question, 'What Good Shall I Do Today?' He then thoughtfully listed in order of their importance the things he wanted to accomplish that day and indicated on his schedule how he would use his time that day for accomplishing his priorities.

Finally, at the top of Franklin's performance maximizing system was his methodology for systematically developing congruence with his thirteen virtues. The right side of his day planner, his 'little book', was the first real-time measurement and feedback system for building character and integrity.

Character/Virtue/Integrity - The Wellsprings of Success

Perhaps Joseph, the son of Jacob of the Old Testament is history's greatest example of the power of character and virtue in achieving success. Sold by his brothers into Egypt, Joseph's remarkable virtue so impressed the Egyptians that he was soon placed in charge of a leading ruler in the Egyptian government by the name of Potiphar. He had complete charge of Potiphar's household, and the ruler's wife soon became enamored of him. Joseph spurned her advances, whereupon she sought to force him to commit adultery with her. Still, he maintained his virtue and fled, she grabbing his cloak to present to her husband as evidence of Joseph's alleged advances toward her. Falsely accused, Joseph was imprisoned, where once again, his integrity and virtue so impressed the jail keeper that he was placed in charge of all of the prisoners.

Eventually, Joseph was brought before Pharaoh to interpret a dream that he had had during the night. Not only did Joseph relate to him what the dream was, but explained to him that the dream was of profound importance to the survival of Egypt. There were to be seven years of abundance and then seven years of famine in the land. The Pharaoh was so impressed that he placed Joseph second in command to himself and instructed him to prepare Egypt to survive the coming seven years of famine.

Joseph's work literally saved the country and blessed the lives of many surrounding countries. His virtue had endowed him with great power and influence in serving his fellow beings. Benj. Franklin knew this story well and knew of the incalculable influence Jesus Christ had had and still has upon the world because of his perfect congruence with the universal laws that pertain to the maximization of personal growth and freedom. He correctly determined that the greatest factor in maximizing his potential for service to his fellow beings was to seek to perfect his character. A hundred and fifty years later, it was noted psychologist, William James, author of the seminal, *Principles of Psychology*, that so insightfully coined the now famous truism, *"Sow a thought, reap and action. Sow an action, reap a habit. Sow habit, reap a character. Sow a character, reap a destiny."*

That virtue is the wellspring of success has been recognized by all of the great leaders of history. While brilliance and ambition can lead one to great heights, without integrity and virtue, there is inevitable self-destruction and resulting loss of the enduring influence for good that brings joy and happiness. Historians all agree that George Washington's ability to lead hungry, ill-equipped soldiers to victory in the American Revolution was the force of his character. So great was his stature that he was almost worshipped by his men.

Benj. Franklin's monumental life is a mighty testament to the power of the 'habitude of virtue'. His motto for his little book and inscribed upon the ivory plates was: *"Here will I hold. If there's a power above us (And that there is, all of nature cries aloud thru all her works,) he must delight in virtue; And that which he delights in must be happy."* Not only did he achieve great congruence with universal principles and his personal *standards of performance,* he also had a *strategy for success.* His success strategy is the subject of the latter part of this chapter.

While none of the companies that have marketed Franklin's time management format have included his self-measurement system, as indicated earlier, there are now at least two smart phone and tablet applications for Implementing Franklin's character development and success maximizing principles. One is called 'Virtues' and the other, Ben's Virtues.

Franklin's Universal Success Principles

As indicated earlier, Benj. Franklin engaged in extensive research to identify a holistic set of principles that would serve as standards of performance for his quest for the achievement of his full potential and that would imbue him with integrity and virtue. His phenomenal track record of service and the avowed felicity of his life should be adequate verification of the validity of his principles. Of course, one's prioritizing of the principles and one's personal values linked to them will differ from Franklin's because of one's uniqueness. But the principles themselves are universal and still represent the most powerful standards for achieving career success ever identified.

Though Franklin's thirteen principles were not wholly without religion, there was in them no mark of any of the distinguishing tenets of any particular sect. He had purposely avoided them. In his own words: *"...for being fully persuaded of the utility and excellency of my method, and that it might be serviceable to people in all religions, and intending some time or other to publish it, I deliberately avoided anything in it that should prejudice anyone, of any sect, against it."*

Temperance

Under the universal success principle of *temperance*, Franklin defined his personal value as *"Eat not to dullness; drink not to elevation"*. For himself, Franklin prioritized Temperance as number one, as it tends to procure that *"coolness and clearness of head which is so necessary where constant vigilance was to be kept up and guard* maintained against the unremitting attraction of ancient habits and the force of perpetual temptation." Like Stephen Covey's "sharpen the saw", in his seminal 7 Habits of Highly Successful People, (it has now sold more than twenty-million copies), Franklin considered physical fitness and clear headedness as step one, and fundamental to enduring success. For someone who does not drink but has a weight problem, the personal value under Temperance might be something like "Limit calorie intake to 1600 per day; exercise at least a half an hour per day".

Silence

"Speak not but what may benefit others or yourself; avoid trifling conversation." Perhaps no other principles is as powerful as the ability to speak only positively of others and to "seek first to understand, then to be understood" as exhorted by Covey's Habit no. 5. Franklin was fond of the saying that "God gave me two ears and only one mouth; it would behoove me to listen twice as much as I talk." Franklin placed this value number two, very near the top because of its great influence in achieving success.

Franklin learned the virtue of silence during his many years as secretary of the Pennsylvania Assembly. Hour after hour, day after day, and month after month he would silently record the proceedings of the Assembly, never expressing the great ideas he often entertained about the governance of the Colony. His faithfulness and diligence gradually gained the respect of every member of the Assembly and eventually, he was invited without any prompting of his own to become a voting member of the Assembly. He then became a powerful agent of change and improvement in the Colony, never seeking credit for his ideas, but rather, often attributing his brilliant ideas to others. The ready reception of his contributions as a result of this practice was a great lesson to him, which he never forgot, and forever after, he attempted to ascribe credit for many of his ideas to others.

Probably no other principle of human psychology is as effective in influencing others as the willingness to genuinely listen, avoid gossip, and seek understanding of others and their ideas and proposals. Only when this quality of character is demonstrated can one maximize the advancement of their worthy ideas.

Order

Let all your things have their places; let each part of your business have its time. Almost everyone has attended a time management seminar. Time management is just fundamental to high achievement and success. During the 1940's an attorney by the name of Morris Perkin was reading Benj. Franklin's autobiography when he came across the graphic of Franklin's time management system. Perkin recognized the validity of Franklin's system and duplicated the left side of his 'little book', creating a page for each day of the year. In place of the right hand side of Franklin's 'little book', the real-time feedback system on character development, Perkin substituted a page divided into fifteen minute intervals for the purpose of tracking his billable time as an attorney. Thus, was born the two pages per day, day planner. Perkin's planner attracted so much attention, that he eventually co-founded the Day-Timers Corporation, which made the planner a national hit with business people.

Eventually, a professor at Columbia University by the name of Charles Hobbs created a highly successful time management seminar using the Day-Timer and some of Franklin's methodology for actualizing personal values. Later The Franklin International Institute, and now a company by the name of FranklinCovey produces a day planner based on the left side of Benj. Franklin's original day planner. Until recently, as mentioned above, no one had modernized and fully restored Franklin's powerful, real-time feedback system.

Resolution

Resolve to perform what you ought; perform without fail what you resolve. Herein, lies the very essence of integrity. Much of success in both life and business is founded in *trust* and *trustworthiness.* When Benj. Franklin, who is often called the *'founder of American business'* opened his print shop in Philadelphia he resolved to never promise what he could not deliver and to always deliver more than he had promised, an additional measure thrown in for good will. This practice quickly gained him a reputation for integrity as a businessman to the extent he soon had more business than he could handle. He was asked to print the colonies' first paper money, the first postage stamps, and did all of the printing for the Philadelphia Assembly over the many years he was its clerk.

Frugality

Make no expense but to do good to yourself or others; that is, waste nothing. Early in his life frugality helped Benj. Franklin obtain books for his self-education in the classics. He only encountered debt once during his lifetime when he was striving to establish his own printing enterprise during his early years in Philadelphia, which he quickly retired by diligent attention to his business. Throughout out his life he lived modestly, preferring rather to invest his money in public enterprise and the general good of the community rather to lavish it upon himself in the form of luxuries, elegant living quarters, or exquisite food.

One of the curses of our modern day society is consumer debt. While debt is appropriate for wise, long term investments, it is never appropriate for short term indulgences and should be avoided like the plague. The avoidance of debt is crucial to enduring success, and frugality has always been a virtue of success-driven people. More will be said of frugality later, as it is not only a virtue, but also a key essential of the Franklin strategy for success.

Industry

"*Lose not time; be always employed in something useful; cut off all unnecessary actions*" Being raised on the edge of poverty, Benj. Franklin learned early the necessity of hard, unrelenting work. He believed this circumstance was no small factor in his determination at a young age to not only learn a craft but also to use all of his discretionary time to educate himself to as full an extent as possible, not being able to attend formal schooling except for a brief time in his early years. So, in addition to attempting to carry more than his share of the load in his brother's print shop, he would often borrow a book and read it entirely through before retiring in the early hours of the morning. In this manner, he exposed himself to the great literature of his time and doubtless laid a foundation for much of the work he was called upon to do in my latter years.

This habit, of always being engaged in something useful, was the key to many discoveries he was privileged to participate in throughout his life. On the many voyages, for example, he made to England, he engaged himself in regular measurements of the ocean's temperatures and eventually gathered enough data to chart what came to be known as the Gulf Stream, which had no small influence on how the North Atlantic ocean was henceforth navigated.

Sincerity

"*Use no harmful deceit; think innocently and justly, and if you speak, speak accordingly.* Nothing is as disarming and refreshing to another person as is *honesty* and *sincerity*. Hidden, selfish agendas are almost always detectable and are harmful of trust, and when one's agenda is genuinely the betterment of his or her fellow beings, great respect is engendered. As a consummately successful diplomat, Benj. Franklin's greatest strength was his honesty and sincerity. His candidness before the British Parliament led to the overturn of the despicable Stamp Act in the American colonies. Later his amazing lack of pretense, arriving in France wearing a coonskin cap, completely captivated the French, and with his honesty and sincerity, he was successful in obtaining from France the help needed for the colonies to win the Revolutionary War.

Another secret of Franklin's astounding success was his early insight that people almost invariably rise to one's expectations of them. He therefore decided that he would naturally trust people, that he would think innocently of them and give them the benefit of the doubt. He never worried much about the theft of his ideas and inventions. He learned that that the best way to have one's ideas gain acceptance of others was to give credit for them to someone else, there seeming to be a natural tendency for others to see that, eventually, credit for both good and bad deeds be attributed to their rightfully author.

Likewise, he sought to speak without duplicity or dogmatism. And while frequently, he held strong views about the topic at hand, still, he would avoid words such as *most certainly, surely, absolutely,* etc., and would substitute, rather, statements such as *I conceive, I apprehend, or I imagine a* thing might be so or so, or it *appears to me at present.* When another asserted something that he thought in error, he would deny himself the pleasure of contradicting him or her abruptly, and of showing immediately some absurdity in his proposition; and in answering he began by observing that *in certain cases or circumstances* his opinion would be right, but in the present case there *appeared* or *secured* to me some difference, etc.

His sincerity, he believed, eventually gained him the confidence of his country, his clients in his business ventures, and was no small factor in the many honorable callings that were conferred upon him throughout his life. Indeed, sincerity is an indispensable habit of one who desires success in life.

Justice

"Wrong none by doing injuries, or omitting the benefits that are your duty." To Franklin it appeared that it was easier to dispense with the virtue of justice when one was hiding behind a mantle of bureaucracy. Often unjust acts toward the common man seemed to be easily be rationalized as being 'official policy' or for the 'good of the whole' at the expense of the individual or because of the false assumption of some 'divine right' one supposedly has to inflict his will upon another. So, he resolved to never use bureaucracy and bad 'policy' as an excuse for failing to secure justice for others. He would either get the bad policy changed or find some other way to secure unto his associates and subordinates the action they deserved.

In positions of authority, it sometimes takes great courage to fight for the rights of individuals rather than to simply submit to bad policy. But there are times when one must lay a career on the line and champion a just cause. And if done with diplomacy and tact, in more cases than not, the hierarchy will respond and gain great respect for the one who respectfully rocked the boat.

Moderation

"Avoid extremes; forbear resenting injuries so much as you think they deserve." As has already been mentioned, Franklin determined at a young age to abandon the dogmatism that often results from too much learning, and no one ever heard a dogmatic expression from him after his mid-twenties. He also desired to avoid grudges and resenting injuries unjustly administered. One such injury, he believed was administered to him by a member of the Pennsylvania Assembly upon his nomination for a second term in this position, a position he had not sought in the first place. He was elected by a unanimous vote except for this one man. He was convinced that Franklin was an arrogant snob and that he had gained too much influence and

admiration of his associates in the Assembly, and the man was active in seeking to destroy his reputation.

Upon learning that this Assemblyman possessed a rare book that he had long desired to read, he wrote him a note requesting a loan of the book, which to his surprise the adversary willingly granted. Upon reading the book, he returned it with a note expressing his appreciation, and noticed shortly thereafter the man's countenance toward him completely changed. They eventually became close friends and remained so until the man's death. This experience convinced Franklin that the best way to deal with an enemy is to asked a favor of him, and then to take the opportunity of making him feel a genuine expression of gratitude toward himself. He learned that few can resist the softening influence of this approach and that often a former enemy can become a truer friend than one whose friendship was not earned in such a guileless manner.

Cleanliness

"Tolerate no uncleanliness in body, clothes, or habitation. In today's society, it is not so much cleanliness that is the issue, but rather, appropriate grooming. 'Clean cut' is still a desirable way to be perceived, even in an environment of 'anything goes'. While professionalism today allows significant diversity, neatness and a modicum of conservatism in dress and grooming still gains one an advantage in the professional workplace.

Tranquility

"Do not be disturbed at trifles, or at accidents, common or unavoidable." Stress and stress management seem to be big issues in today's world. Franklin learned quickly from his experience in trying to get to Philadelphia the first time and from subsequent, numerous

crossings of the Atlantic Ocean that storms are a natural part of navigation both of ships and of life and that the best practice is to view them as experiences necessary to the development of character.

One needs develop a high degree of 'equanimity' to avoid excessive stress. The popular saying of the day is *'It is 10% what happens to you, and 90 % how you handle it.'* That is because we often do not choose our adverse circumstances, but we do have a choice of how react to them.

The famous Victor Frankl, author of *Man's Search for Meaning,* demonstrated that even in a German concentration camp, one can find meaning and purpose through selfless service to others who have found themselves in the same circumstances and survive all the better for having endured adversity. His experiences in this environment led him to eventually found an entirely new field of psychology call *logo therapy.*

Chastity

The only thing that can be said of chastity in our libertine society is that one should search deeply within their own soul, listen to the still small voice of their conscience, and seek to do the right thing. There is a moral code on the issue of sexuality, inspired of Providence. Discovering and adhering to this code is absolutely crucial to enduring success. Violating this code has probably destroyed more careers and caused more emotional suffering than any other aspect of human performance. It is the responsibility of each individual to live up to the light has been placed in each one of us by our Creator. It goes without saying that abstaining from the viewing of pornagrphy is absolutely essential to the maintaining of chastity.

Humility

"Imitate Jesus and Socrates." Franklin's list of virtues contained at first but twelve, but a Quaker friend, having kindly informed him that he was generally thought proud, that his pride showed itself frequently in conversation, that he was not content with being in the right when discussing any point, but was overbearing and rather insolent, of which his Quaker friend convinced him by mentioning several instances, he determined to cure himself, if possible, of this vice or folly among the rest, and so, he added *Humility* to his list, giving an extensive meaning to the word, and has related earlier, he went about overcoming his early overbearingness.

Jim Collins, author of the best selling book, Good to Great, when asked in an interview with Fortune Magazine, "...what do you feel is the most important quality in a successful business leader?" answered: "Willful humility." The best CEOs in our research display tremendous ambition for their company combined with the stoic will to do whatever it takes, no matter how brutal (within the bounds of the company's core value), to make the company great. Yet at the same they display a remarkable humility about themselves, ascribing much of their own sucecss to luck, discipline, and preparation rather than personal genius."

When Benj. Franklin wrote his autobiography at age seventy-nine, he said, *"I cannot boast of much success in acquiring the reality of this virtue, but I had a good deal with regard to the appearance of it. In reality, there is, perhaps, no one of our national passions so hard to subdue as pride. Disguise it, struggle with it, beat it down, stifle, it, mortify it as much as one pleases, it is still alive and will every now and then peep out and show itself; you will see it, perhaps, often in my history, for, even if I could conceive that I had completely overcome it, I should probably be proud of my humility"*.

Personal Values

The definition of one's personal values as pertaining to each of the success principles should be carefully thought out so as to clearly define performance standards for shaping one's character. Franklin's principles are still as valid today for achieving success as they were in his day. But given the reality that each person is at a different stage of character development and each has different perceptions of what constitutes *temperance, silence, order,* etc., it is important to engage in a significant interval of introspection during which clarity of one's values emerges. Thus, one might want to keep some of Franklin's definitions and to customize others.

For example, if one has already achieved a high degree of organization in their business life, the principle of *order,* might be defined rather as, *achieve and maintain greater organization of personal possessions and finances; implement a workable budget system for personal and/or family financial matters.*

Inasmuch as one frequently encounters situations where there are two right choices in a particular circumstance, one's principles and values should be prioritized. For example, there might be an occasion where the purchase of an electronic device for logging, tracking, and analyzing purchase receipts and expenditures might of significant benefit to the value of *order* as defined above, but that might conflict the principle of *frugality.* Based on how one's values are defined and prioritized, a decision could be made that would optimize one's quest for greater success in life.

Early in Benjamin Franklin's life, he determined to become a vegetarian, eating no meat or fish, a practice which he observed for an extended period of time. Upon fleeing his brothers' print shop, having been found out and beaten for his deceptive 'Silence Dogood' essays, he found himself on a boat heading for Philadelphia. Being by this time very hungry, when the captain offered him some fish, he cheerfully accepted it, deeming his immediate health and well being of greater value than his commitment to vegetarianism.

Let not the above counsel be misinterpreted as *situational ethics,* however. There are some values that are part of one's moral code that must not be violated under any condition. If one's religion, for example, forbids the partaking of alcoholic beverages, there are no circumstances under which this value should be violated. One will find that in such circumstances the possible immediate disapproval of this kind of self-denial by those preferring such spirits will almost always engender long term respect and admiration within those same people.

Congruence – the Source of Power

If virtue is the wellspring of success, *congruence* is the source of power. Character requires connecting one's values to universal principles, and then achieving unity with these values. Congruence is defined as the amount of alignment between one's values and one's behavior. Success results from living in harmony with truth and values and following a clearly defined and proven strategy for maximizing personal and career potential. As indicated earlier, it was the achievement of his congruence with universal success principles and personal values using his 'little book' to which Benj. Franklin, toward the end of his life, attributed the large measure of his happiness and success.

In his audiocassette series, *The Insight System for Managing Your Time and Your Life,* Dr. Charles Hobbs introduced the idea of *concentration of power.* The mind is a lens through which we see the world. Stephen Covey is fond of saying, "*we do not see the world as it is, but as we are.*" Congruence with one's values, which have been based on universal truths and principles, brings values and behavior, like two magnifying lenses, into focus. The greater our focus, the more we see the world as it is and the more our influence on that world grows. As the harmony between our values and behavior approaches completeness, we develop power and influence over our circumstances. We achieve a high degree of wholeness, unity, and completeness, which is also called *integrity*.

Achieving congruence is so important to character and career success that Benj. Franklin felt it necessary to actually measure his congruence with his values. The problem, however with his system was that it was based entirely *on negative* feedback. While the system worked well for him, most of us do better with positive feedback systems. The smart phone and tablet applications mentioned earlier provide a choice of generating either negative or positive feedback. One of Stephen Covey's 7 Habits of Highly Successful People is *"Be proactive."* He teaches that each of us has a circle of influence and in order to be highly effective our effort must be focused on circumstances and events within that circle. As we master the circumstances within this circle, the circle begins to naturally grow larger. Excelling at the job at hand, regardless of what that job is the route to an ever expanding circle of influence and leadership. As one develops congruence and personal integrity and takes each project and excels at that task no matter how mundane, one's circle of influence grows. Eventually, using this process, one becomes a *leader*. It is ultimately this process coupled with real-time feedback on performance in the workplace that will lead to a maximization of life success.

The Principles of Process Control

In the late 1930's the principles of statistical process control (SPC) were developed at Bell Laboratories. These principles were a huge factor in the industrial miracle that made victory in WW II possible. Following WW II, men such as W. Edwards Deming and Joseph Juran sought to teach the principles of statistical process control to U.S business leaders, moving from war production to the production of consumer goods. Perhaps, not surprisingly, U.S. business, seeking to supply the mushrooming demand of the newly liberated world for modern conveniences, could only think in terms of volume of output, quality largely going out the window. There was now little interest in quality control in America.

So Deming, Juran, and a small band of other pioneers were called to Japan by General Douglas McArthur to help rebuild its manufacturing capacity and to instill quality into the notoriously poor Japanese products. The Japanese were ready to listen, and soon almost every Japanese manufacturing industry was utilizing the principles of SPC. By the late 1960's Japan was leading a world wide revolution in manufacturing quality and productivity. Here are the principles of SPC:

- Clearly defined quality standards
- Real-time, self-measurement of product quality
- Graphical feedback on results
- Continuous improvement of process quality

Deming defined productivity as *process quality* instead of the worker speed. He found that 90% of productivity problems were problems with the process and not the people and that once the process was right the output was pretty well automatic. The reason productivity = process quality rather than speed is that if the process is right there is dramatically less waste and fewer rejects and redo's. Instead of counting the number of defective products off the line, defects are detected quickly during the manufacturing process, the process fixed, and the defects prevented instead of having to be fixed after leaving the process.

Benj. Franklin's real-time feedback system on adherence to universal success standards was a remarkably advanced application of SPC in the area of the maximization of career success. Unfortunately, the restorers of Franklin's time management system have failed to modernize and bring forth this powerful tool. Neither has Franklin's system and SPC been implemented in the knowledge work environment, and most knowledge work processes are as a result, significantly under-performing. Only recently has the software been developed to bring the power of SPC to knowledge work. The principles are the same, and finally, Franklin's and Deming's pioneering work can be tapped to move to achieving peak performance both in the life success and the knowledge workplace. Peak performance in the work place is covered in Appendix V of this work.

Having thoroughly covered Benj. Franklin's career success principles and methodology for developing the habits of success, let us now take a more in depth look at his lifetime strategy for maximizing career success.

Scholarship

Benj. Franklin's life followed five clearly identifiable phases in his becoming the paragon of personal productivity for all time. The first of those phases is *scholarship*. There is nothing new here. It is self-evidently true that the early years of life must be largely dedicated to building a data base of knowledge and developing the ability and discipline to process that data. But Benj. Franklin's early life is a monument to the value of a balanced and holistic, three-fold educational strategy.

One, of course, must apply one's self diligently to meeting a high standard in formal instruction, to *studying hard in curriculum and career.* But often neglected in the early years is the crucial independent and self-guided *survey of the classics,* especially the Old and New Testaments. One cannot consider him or herself *educated* without having delved deeply into the Bible. Probably, the most sublime and ennobling of all literature is David's book of Psalms. The most prolific condensation of wisdom ever recorded is found in the book of Proverbs. The founding fathers of our nation cited more than three thousand references to the contents of the Bible in their framing of the Constitution of the United States. Indeed the moral decay of our society can largely be attributed from the loss of a grounding in Biblical teachings, that was so pervasive in the early history of our country and indeed until the secularization of our society that began in earnest in the early part of the twentieth century.

The Book of Ecclesiastes describes Solomon's search for the meaning of life, by his own unaided intellect and apart from divine revelation. His conclusion was that without God, life is vanity and as futile as chasing the wind. The Song of Solomon is one of the great primers on romantic love and sexual relations between man and woman. The Bible is one of the few sources of the ancient history of the world. History's greatest philosopher, Jesus Christ, is quoted extensively and his biography and teachings are contained in the New Testament.

The very foundations of England's Common Law and the U.S.'s constitution and form of government are derived from Moses' governance of the children of Israel after the exodus. Indeed the devastating loss of our moral compass as a nation and a world is because of the failure of now several generations to have grown up without a thorough grounding in the Bible.

Benj. Franklin was schooled at the feet of the great Cotton Mather and studied the Bible thoroughly in his youth. But he balanced this education with an extraordinarily wide exposure to the great classics of early history. At the age of sixteen, as an apprentice in his brother James' print shop Benj. gained access to books from the libraries of the shop's clientele and to important publications from England, such as *The Spectator,* which he used to teach himself to write. As indicated in the Preface, he studied the great philosophers of history. He would read well into the early morning hours. He persuaded James to give him the money James was spending for his board and then halved that expenditure, applying the other half to the purchase of books, eating only a biscuit and some raisins for lunch. And while young Benj. had to go to great lengths to acquire his liberal arts education, today a full text, thousand volume library of the classics can be purchased on a single CD for $19.95. With almost every individual now with a P.C., notebook or tablet computer, there is simply no excuse for one not surveying and studying the great philosophers of history. This study was an important foundation for his contributions to the formulation in the last years of his life of the Constitution of the United States.

Scholarship

Supremacy in Some Niche of Knowledge

Spend Time with the Bbile & the Classics

Study Hard n Curriculum &

Finally, scholarship involves becoming the world's authority in some niche of knowledge. Such was the case with Benj. Franklin's search for universal values by which to shape his character and his search for an understanding of the nature of electricity. Likewise, so thorough was his research into and innovation in personal performance, the time management half of his 'little book' formulated in 1731 still serves as the basis for the most successful time management systems on the market today, such as the Day-Timers and FranklinCovey day planners (now mostly in the electronic format). Not until recently, though, has his expertise in real-time graphical feedback on performance for acceleration of the achievement of life success, finally been adapted for modern day use, via the earlier mentioned software applications..

So pioneering (for that day and age) was Franklin's work in electricity, many of its attributes still bear the names he gave them more than 250 years ago, such as *positive* and *negative charges, battery, capacitor,*and *'grounding'*. As mentioned earlier, for this work, he was awarded the Copley Gold Metal, inducted in the Royal Society of London, and awarded several honorary doctorate degrees. Remarkably, a printer with a mere eight months of formal education, by life threatening experimentation and an exhaustive study of he existing literature on electricity became the world's authority in that eventual revolutionary technology.

One might initially recoil at the imposing challenge of becoming the world's authority in some niche of knowledge. But such an achievement is not as unfathomable as it first appears. First of all, most of the competition is watching TV or playing video games. The serious researcher is rare indeed in today's world. Secondly, the existence of the World Wide Web, which provides instant access to more than eight billion web sites, makes research almost infinitely easier than in Franklin's day.

When one genuinely becomes the world's authority on something, the world sits up and pays attention, for fifteen minutes, at least. Such is the case with Monty Roberts who wrote the book on the language and behavior of horses. Roberts was raised by a dad that used violence to tame unbroken horses.

Such behavior repulsed Monty Roberts, and he began at a young age to learn the language of horses how to train them without violence. Eventually, he became the world's authority on changing horse behavior with kindness. His expertise was so thorough that he eventually accepted a challenge to capture and place a saddle on a wild Mustang horse without using force.

In less than twenty-four hours, Monty successfully saddled and mounted a rider on the Mustang without a single use of force. Monty is now wealthy and famous, and just as Benj. Franklin did with his wealth and fame, he has dedicated his life to serving his fellow beings through the rehabilitation of rebellious horses and wayward boys.

In summary, scholarship is a dedicated pursuit of the knowledge necessary to fully develop one's unique potential for service. It begins with at least twelve years of formal schooling and in most cases another four to six or eight years. It requires, in addition, a personal independent quest for genuine authority in some subject and the higher level of knowledge, holism, and balance that comes with learning from the great philosophers, writers, and poets of history.

Finally, one's education continues for a lifetime and even afterwards, one's work to come forth again, as Benj. Franklin so accurately perceived upon what he thought was his death bed during a relatively early life serious illness "*...the Work shall not be Lost; For it will Appear once More, In a New and More Elegant Edition, Revised and Corrected, By the Author.*"

Skills

The steep rise in unemployment in the U.S. beginning in the first decade of this century has revealed once again the importance of cutting edge skills if one is to survive and prosper in lean times. In negative business cycles being the best at one's specialty is the only way to avoid the inevitable layoffs and downsizing as companies cut costs in order to survive.

So, while one must very early in life dedicate him or herself to a lifetime of diligent scholarship, there must also be a concurrent development of world class skills in some field of endeavor. At the age of twelve, Josiah apprenticed his son Benj., at his request, to his brother James to learn the craft of printing. Franklin maximized this opportunity by exploiting his proximately to great books and literature at the print shop to continue his scholarship, while at the same time diligently applying himself to the acquisition of a high degree of skill in the printing business. Upon fleeing James' flogging for the Silence Dogood affair, he was unable to find work in New York and ended up in the progressive city of Philadelphia.

With his already high degree of skill in printing he soon found work in a print shop there, where he proceeded to make it the cutting edge printing business in the city. By his early twenties, he owned his own printing business and proceeded to become recognized as the best printer in the Colonies. He literally *became* the cutting edge printer in America with numerous innovations and extraordinary customer service. He then began to acquire printing operations in a number of other colonies and territories. Even though he lacked a formal education and faced difficult economic times, he was financial secure by the age of 42.

So, step one in developing world class skills is to *select a skilled mentor*, then, ask a lot of questions and listen carefully. Most experts in a field love to share what they know and upon sensing a deep desire of one to learn from them, they will pour out their hearts and derive great satisfaction from seeing their student grow and develop. All great achievers have had great mentors even as all great athletes have had great coaches.

Then, one must *scour the field for best practices*. There are islands of excellence in every field of endeavor, and one must find these unique and special operations and learn from them. Most of them will freely share their secrets of success. Additionally, there are a number of best practice institutes and plenty of information on the Internet about the latest developments in a given field.

Finally, one must, with missionary zeal dedicate him or herself to becoming the cutting edge in the business. One must determine to become the world's authority in his or her field. While this challenge might seem imposing and even unrealistic, making the effort will elicit the best that one has to offer and assure that one's contribution and value to his or her organization is maximized. And there is nothing more assuring of job security in lean times than cutting edge performance. The mediocre do not survive the downsizing in negative business cycles.

Solvency

Life can really be fun if all of all of one's energy is not consumed in trying to subsist. To become financially independent at a young age should be every person's goal so that the rest of their life can be spent in service, doing what they were uniquely born to do. And there is a simple formula for achieving financial success. It is: *spend frugally, shun debt,* and *save and invest regularly.* Savings, of course, includes investing wisely, including benevolence even in the lean years. Everyone has heard of the power of compound interest. And everyone has heard the truism that *"Give, and it shall be given unto you; good measure, pressed down, and shaken together, and running over, shall men give into your bosom."*

If one could but learn to live on 20% less than their income, 10% allocated to savings and 10% to benevolence, one could easily be financially independent by the age of forty-five. Billionaire Jon Huntsman tells of how he and his young wife, from the very beginning of their marriage, while they were struggling through college, allocated $50 a month to charitable causes, *after* tithing their income to their church. He said he believes that that benevolence was a key ingredient in his eventual rise to great success, financially.

James Ritchie of The Ritchie Group Real Estate Investments employed a similar strategy. He and his wife spent frugally in the early years, invested in wise business ventures, gave liberally from the beginning of their marriage, and were financially secure by their mid-thirties. They have now spent the last thirty years of their lives serving their fellow beings, world wide, most recently, with four years of service in a poor African country. Their lives have been filled with joy from the service that they have been able to render because of their following the formula for financial success early in their lives.

The greatest secret to rising to the top in any endeavor is to take the task at hand, regardless of how mundane, and excel at it. One need not concern him or herself with promotions, pay, or position. These things will come naturally and rapidly if one will but do the job at hand better than it has ever been done before. Such was Benj. Franklin's first printing job in Philadelphia. Samuel Keimer agreed to let Benj. Franklin help him with printing an elegy, Franklin noted the plainness of Keimer's work and also that there was an unused and non-functional press in Keimer's shop. He immediately repaired the old press, acquired some new type and printed the elegy, putting a border around it and dramatically improving its appearance. Keimer was so impressed that he hired Benj. on full time and pretty well put him in charge. Within a few years, Benj. Franklin owned his own printing business and became Philadelphia and the Colonies' leading printer.

Noted business man Larry Miller (now deceased) of Salt Lake City began as a parts clerk in a car dealership in Colorado. He excelled at the job, rose to the top and become the owner of numerous car dealerships, the Utah Jazz, and many other successful enterprises.

Mark Cuban, young billionaire and owner of the Dallas Mavericks decided to tackle the blossoming computer industry despite having no background knowledge of the subject. Cuban founded MicroSolutions, a computer consulting firm, in 1983, which went on to become National Systems Integrator. By 1990, his company was grossing $30 million per year. He sold the business toe CompuServe for hundreds of millions of dollars and then went on to found Broadcast.com, now a major player in multi-media and online sports.

In summary, there are simple principles (admittedly difficult to apply) that will guarantee financial security at an early age. Even if one is not entrepreneurial, any mundane job can be turned in to a rapid rise to the top. Any job is bigger than the person in it, and initiative, innovation, and excelling at the job will always open the doors to greater opportunity. Then, one needs only to take the next job and excel at it. Highly structured, short, intermediate, and long term goals are not needed. One needs a vision of financial independence and service and uncommon dedication to the task at hand. Frugality, savings, investments, and benevolence will take care of the rest.

Self-Actualization

Abraham Maslow, in his seminal work, *Toward a Psychology of Being,* elegantly identified the essentials of the high-achieving individual with his needs hierarchy model of human behavior. In hundreds of interviews with high-achieving individuals he identified the principle motivators of human behavior in ascending order: the need for *safety* (or security), for *belonging,* for *love* and *esteem,* and finally, the need for what he called *self-actualization* (the progressive realization of one's special mission in life).

Maslow discovered that the motivating strength of the first four of the fundamental human needs decline as they are progressively satisfied. The motivating strength of the highest order need, self-actualization, he found however, gains strength as it is experienced. Once the individual discovers what it is that he or she is uniquely born to do, what actualizes his or her true potential, his or her personal mission in life, the doing of it is no longer work, but play, although it typically elicits the most arduous expenditure of energy on the part of the individual.

One of the things Benj. Franklin was born to do was to define the nature of lightning and to write the book on electricity. Having done that and having gained world wide fame from it, he then spent the rest of his life in statesmanship and diplomacy.

He was still self-actualizing at the age of eighty-two when he returned from France to play a major role in bringing forth the Constitution of the United States.

Not everyone has such a major role to play in bringing the dream of freedom to life, but everyone has something that only they can do. And the greatest joy in life comes from discovering one's special gift and giving that gift to one's fellow beings. How does one discover that special thing they were born to do better than anyone has ever been done it before? Every one has something that piques their interest, that they day dream about. One of the questions that can elicit a focus on that special thing is *"What would I do with my time if I had all the money in the world?"* or, *"If I were going to write a book, what would it be about?"*

J.K. Rowling was a destitute single mother when she hearkened to her inner voice and began to write about Harry Potter and his 'wizard' adventures. After many rejections she finally succeeded in getting her first Harry Potter book published in 1997. She has now built a billion dollar empire with her books and the resulting movies and promotions based on her work.

Of course, most of us will not become a super-star and earn hundreds of millions of dollars, but all of us can discover our special gift and self-publish our work for the benefit of others. It should be our life's mission to give our special gift. And having gained financial independence, we will have the wherewithal to give this gift for the benefit of others in a life of service doing what we love most.

Service

Noted business man, public servant, and cleric, the late, N. Eldon Tanne,r was fond of saying, *"service is the rent we pay for living in this world of ours."* Benj. Franklin's morning prayers to his God included this statement: *"Accept my kind offices to thy children as the only return in my power for thy continual favors toward me."* Indeed success might be defined as achieving the ability to maximize one's contribution to the betterment of his or her fellow beings.

Nothing else in life brings joy like a selfless service. Indeed, a strategy for success is a strategy that is designed to free one to serve and to develop one's full potential for building the dream of freedom for mankind. Covey crystallizes the purpose of life as *"to live, to learn, to love, to leave a legacy"*, meaning a legacy of service and integrity. If anything characterizes Benj. Franklin's life, it was service. In his early twenties he formed what he called the 'Junta', an association for self-betterment and for brainstorming ideas for the improvement of society.

Out of Franklin's Junta came the first circulating library in America, the first hospital, the first secular university, the American

Philosophical Society, the first fire insurance company (which still exists today), some of the first street lights in America, the first environmental protection association, the first voluntary fire department, and many other improvements that revolutionized life in Philadelphia and eventually, the Colonies.

His *Poor Richard's Almanac,* widely distributed in America for twenty-five years, was next to the churches and the Bible, the most important of all influences that shaped the founding values of America. His inventions and innovations improved the air quality, health, safety, culinary quality, transportation, postal service, politics, meteorology, diplomacy, and ultimately the very freedom, prosperity, and independence of the new nation of America.

Not only is service the wellspring of joy, it is a long term life insurance policy: *"Then shall the King say unto them on his right hand, Come, ye blessed of my Father, inherit the kingdom prepared for you from the foundation of the world: For I was an hungred, and ye gave me meat: I was thirsty, and ye gave me drink: I was a stranger, and ye took me in: Naked, and ye clothed me: I was sick, and ye visited me: I was in prison, and ye came unto me. Then shall the righteous answer him, saying, Lord, when saw we thee an hungred, and fed thee? or thirsty, and gave thee drink? When saw we thee a stranger, and took thee in? or naked, and clothed thee? Or when saw we thee sick, or in prison, and came unto thee ?And the King shall answer and say unto them, Verily I say unto you, Inasmuch as ye have done it unto one of the least of these my brethren, ye have done it unto me."* (Matt. 25:34-40)

Service must include, first of all, service to one's own family. Noted teacher, author, and cleric, the late, David O. McKay, frequently emphasized that: *"No other success can compensate for failure in the home."* Rearing of a virtuous and achieving family is job one for anyone wishing to claim success in this life.

Then, there is service to the community and country. Liberty and the dream of freedom are works in progress. America is not yet built, and every person has a contribution and an obligation to continue the work begun by our founding fathers.

Just as important, however, as the grand work of bringing the dream of freedom to life for a family, a community, and a nation is the anonymous service each of us should continuously render to the ordinary, the aged, the underprivileged, the unrecognized, and the downtrodden. Small, random acts of kindness are no small part of our mission in this life. A smile, an encouraging word, an act of recognition of the many nameless and humble servants that empty our trash, stock our store shelves, sweep our floors, and provide the myriads of other services that make our life better, are the kinds of service that constitute the rent we as citizens of the human family owe for the privilege of living in America, the land of opportunity.

Conclusion

Too many success seminars and self-help books have focused primarily on goal setting and time management while neglecting universal principles, graphical feedback, and the trail-blazing strategy and fifteen-step process that characterized Benj. Franklin's monumental life of extraordinary achievement and service.

Even with the ultimate success system, however, the route to one's special dream of freedom and vision of leaving a legacy of unique value will always be adequately strewn with adversity and failure. The maximization of one's potential simply requires some time in the furnace of affliction. This refining process is essential for the burning out the dross and extracting the gold that lies at the core of every human being. It is adversity that rings the liberty bell, and every one's bell is going to have in it, a small crack. For some of us that crack is a gapping fissure.

The U.S liberty bell was first cast in England and shipped to the country by boat. But it cracked so badly upon being rung the first few times, it had to be melted down, shipped back to England and recast. Even the recast liberty bell developed a crack. But still, it was rung on George Washington's 100th birthday and has since inspired millions who have traveled to Philadelphia to see and touch it.

Likewise, any successful life will have some flaws and failures along the way. Indeed, it is accurate to say that success is built on failure. Benj. Franklin's phenomenal career was for example, launched when he finally admitted to his brother that he had been the author of the popular 'Silence Dogood' essays. He had been deceptively and anonymously slipping them under the print shop door stop, a clear violation of the principle forthrightness with one's boss. So irate was his brother James about this deception, that he physically beat Benj. Franklin, the incident that caused him to abandon his apprenticeship, pack up his knap sack, and depart, first for New York and then Philadelphia. He then proceeded to literally revolutionize life in colonies with his innovative ideas and pioneering solutions to difficult life in the C olonies

One cannot find better role models for career and life success than Benj. Franklin and Stephen Covey. It is not surprising that Franklin's portrait is viewed millions of times a day on the hundred dollar bill. In fact, the hundred dollar bill has become known as 'the

Franklin'. Even today there are hundreds of successful businesses named after him. His life deserves to be studied diligently and his system of developing integrity and virtue should be applied to every career pursuit. He had both a strategy and a system. He consciously chose to be the role model for all time of the super-achiever, and he strongly recommended that those wishing to maximize their life success follow his example.

Stephen Covey who recently passed away at the age of seventy-nine was voted one of the twentieth century's one hundred most influential people. He personally trained executives in almost every one of the Fortune 500 companies as well as thousands of other companies. His books have positively affected the lives of millions of people throughout the world. One must couple his insights, tools, and techniques with Franklin's in order to maximize one's freedom and influence for good in this life.

It is hoped that the new organizational science introduced in this work can now soon join with Franklin's and Covey's work to help bring about a new plateau of human performance in the workplace and to help people maximize personal freedom and life fulfillment during this mortal sojourn.

APPENDICES

APPENDIX I
The DSL Model

✦

With the integrated theory of business and the DSL model, it is now possible for executives and people in all orbits of the organization to identify every essential element of their part of the business, to prioritize the developmental needs of that part of the business, to continually improve performance, and to finally achieve genuine balance in organizational performance.

While Reengineering and Total Quality Management were effective strategies for organizational improvement, they required outside consultants to apply; as soon as the consultants left, generally, their use ceased. The tools and techniques were too complex for the general population of the organization to become comfortable with. The use of the DSL model, by contrast, is sublimely simple.

But the model is so powerful and leads to solutions so rapidly that its use must be tempered with extensive sharing of experiences of the users of the model during the problem-solving session. In using it, the growth and development of the people must be the paramount, the solutions derived simply as a means of building people. The model is based upon three principles.

The first of these is the number *seven*, a natural number of completeness. The number seven has been used extensively in business models, such as in McKinsey's 7-S Framework, which also used another of the basics of the model, the device of alliteration. All of the aspects of organizational behavior in this model, for example, begin with the letter *S*: skills, staffing, style, strategy, structure, systems, and shared values.

The DSL model uses these two basics, the number <u>seven</u> and alliteration, but it adds a third dimension, that of hierarchy in its application of Dynamics, Essentials, and Elements. The model also employs a more intuitive metaphor, a ship with sails and uses alliteration a great deal more extensively. For example, in the *Dynamics of Developmentship,* all of the dynamics begin with a *D,* all of the *essentials* with an *S,* and all of the elements with an *L.*

A broader application of the model and the powerful devices it employs is in the development of the hierarchical aspects of the Seven Determinants of Global Competitiveness. For example, with *Oceans of Opportunity,* all of the aspects of opportunity start with the letter *O* (offshore market opportunities, orbital technologies, etc.).

Taking the solution further, one of the seven Dynamics of Oceans of Opportunity is Developmental Marketing. Then, one of the derived Essentials of Developmental Marketing is, *market segments* might have seven niches that all begin with the letter *N.* Micromarket niches might include nonprofit organizations, novice drivers, new parents, novel pet owners, non–meat eaters, northernmost states, or Nordic skiers. Another, the new Internet markets, and so forth. Marketing executives at another organization, using this model, will identify entirely different market segments for their business.

Over a number of years of using this powerful model of online marketing, ongoing improvements in customer service, obvious gaps in existing markets, and other distribution methods in actual business problem-solving sessions, it became abundantly clear that people come together not just to solve problems, but also to satisfy social agendas and psychological needs. It is crucial therefore, that in any problem-solving session, it is made clear that the people, their development, growth, and sociality are paramount—and the business solution is the natural by-product of skillful modeling and gently applied structure in the synergizing process.

American workers, if anything, are freedom-loving people; to constrict their freedom in structured ways, a problem-solving facilitator must fully validate the problem-solving approach with some background and examples of its success in similar situations.

The DSL model grew out of an approach that Tom Peters and Bob Waterman used to construct their "happy atom" while consultants for the McKinsey Group in the late '70s and early '80s. They used their model in analyzing literally hundreds of organizations in their research for *In Search of Excellence*. The model became known as one of the most effective of the many analytical tools used by consultants. The model was crucial to their finally identifying "shared values" as the central attribute of all of the top-performing companies they studied.

McKinsey's Use of Alliteration and the Number Seven

McKINSEY 7-S FRAMEWORK ©

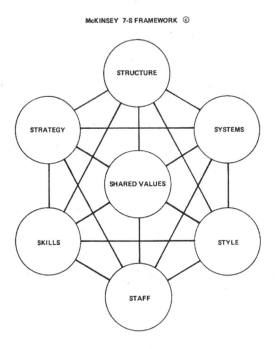

Other letters can be used. In developing, for example, the *oceans of opportunity* further, the team might select *M* for Market Segments, instead of *S*. All the essentials would begin with *M*. For example, offshore markets might include micromarket niches, mass market publications, middle-aged populations, men-only markets, miss-only markets, minor age markets, and mature age markets. It should be pointed out at this juncture that the number seven is only a guideline. There might be a great deal more aspects to a solution for a specific organization—or fewer in some cases.

It can be seen that, by using this tool, all the market segments and possible niches for a specific organization would eventually be identified. By prioritizing these segments and niches and developing action plans for the highest-priority markets, the organization can achieve its full marketing potential. When derived solutions are prioritized, specific actions are planned for the developmental needs of the organization, and actions taken are reported in a team setting, the effects are dramatic. The model provides a simple, effective *structure for synergy*. It is a strategy for daily online collaboration and weekly team meetings that yields continuous improvement in organizational performance.

The DSL model is the first tool that makes possible a comprehensive and holistic approach to organization development. Its use requires little or no training and works just as well for executives as for people at the front line. When applied throughout an organization, it can revolutionize performance.

Discovering the Power of the DSL Model

Peters and Waterman's relate how McKinsey's 7-S Framework© seemed to be hocus-pocus, but it yielded a model that proved to be highly useful in analyzing the effectiveness of organizations worldwide. They related how they had to think deeply to get all of the elementsof the model to start with the letter *S*.

Using alliteration, they accurately identified six crucial essentials of organizational analysis. The number, seven, a number of completeness, required a seventh essential; at the heart of their model, they wanted to convey the powerful influence of organizational values. Using alliteration resulted in identifying the word *shared*. Thus, the values became "shared values." This concept carried a great deal more meaning and power than mere "values." Indeed, alliteration appears to embody unique derivational qualities. Probably no other words in the English language could have expressed the facets of organizational effectiveness as clearly as *structure, strategy, style, systems, skills, staffing,* and *shared values.*

Similarly, in deriving the dynamics of developmentship for the new integrated theory of business, no other words could have conveyed the meanings as well as *dream, determination, drive, discipline, diligence, daring, and dedication.* Using the derivational power of alliteration, it was possible to derive the seven essentials of each dynamic. The dream, for example, consists of sea-changing mission, shared, heroic vision, strong, character-shaping values, supercharging strategy, spherical structure, scintillating symbolism, supporting, soft and hard organizational metrics, and stretching, strategic objectives.

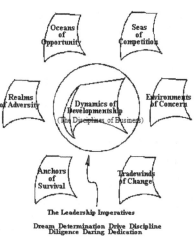

The External Contingencies and
Internal Dynamics of a Business

This author, in working with this literary device extensively in deriving the essentials of business over a twenty-year period, has become convinced that the device is not just apparent magic but a genuine derivational principle that will elicit the deepest of insights.

Of course, Pareto charts, fishbone diagrams, root-cause analysis, and all of the many other tools of Total Quality Management are still valid and should be used in improving organizational performance. With the identification and articulation of the seven dynamics and forty-nine essentials of business, it is possible to maximize business performance.

The number seven leads to holism, bringing about the realization that the dream consists of more than just mission, vision, and values.

And finally, the concept of hierarchy provides the proper sequence of the essentials.

Deriving the seven elements of each essential is, with sufficient mental effort and brainstorming, readily accomplished using the letter *L*. And, while at the strategic level of the organization, such detail may not be needed, this kind of detail becomes important as the model is pushed outward throughout the organization where people are analyzing and improving their jobs, collaboratively and online, in ever-increasing comprehensiveness and holism.

One of the objections to using the DSL model is the perception by users that the constraints imposed by the requirement of the use of certain letters for the various determinants of global competitiveness and of the dynamics, essentials, and elements, of business unnecessarily limits their creative energy. And while this constraint may at first cause discomfort and irritation, after the skill of alliteration is developed, users find the model empowering and fun to use. This methodology does, however, require a great deal more mental effort than most people have been used to in brainstorming sessions; it is helpful to have a skillful facilitator to guide the use of the methodology in the first two or three team sessions in which it is being utilized.

An interesting effect of using the model is that once people become familiar with the methodology, high-quality solutions quickly emerge—so fast, in fact, that people may doubt their validity. Additionally, it became apparent to the author, after extensive use of the model, that people are not just seeking high-quality solutions, but a number of psychological needs that have to do with recognition, esteem, sharing of experiences related to the identified essentials, and team dynamics. For this reason, the use of the model must be tempered with extensive sharing of experiences related to the solution by the participants and recognition of each participant for their contributions to the solutions. Once again, facilitators must remember that the person is the product of collaboration and the solution the by-product.

The author has used the model at all levels of organizations. In one large plant, blue-collar craftsmen were asked to develop behavioral standards for their craft using the model. They became adept at its use during the very first session and completed a very difficult task—one probably never done before—in a matter of three relatively short sessions.

But at progressively higher levels of organizations, the initial resistance to structured thinking can be hampering unless sufficient background and explanation of the model is offered. For example, asking executives to identify the oceans of opportunities available to the organization, using only O words, will probably meet considerable resistance unless it can be sufficiently established that this methodology is a derivational principle essential to the use of an integrated theory of business (the Seven Determinants of Global Competitiveness).

The newness of the DSL model requires that users demonstrate some humility and initially exhibit faith in the alliteration methodology. The evidence that the principles are based upon have long been used with noteworthy success in the derivation of highly useful solutions in many areas of endeavor. A conviction of the validity of the integrated theory of business and the DSL model soon comes with the clarity, holism, and balanced perspective of the organization that arises out of the use of the model.

In summary, there are several reasons for the power of the DSL model and methodology in analyzing the effectiveness of the organization. First of all, it is an essential part of an integrated theory of business. Secondly, it is the only model available today that allows a completely holistic, comprehensive, and balanced analysis of an organization. Thirdly, its solutions emanate from the organization's own people and not from consultants. Fourthly, it is based on three well-validated principles: alliteration, the number of completeness (7), and the principle of hierarchy or priority. And finally, it utilizes graphical metaphors that harmonize with deeply held cultural norms, those of a pioneering voyage in quest of the dream of freedom, the desire for the full development of one's productive potential, and the desire for global competitiveness in the realm of human enterprise.

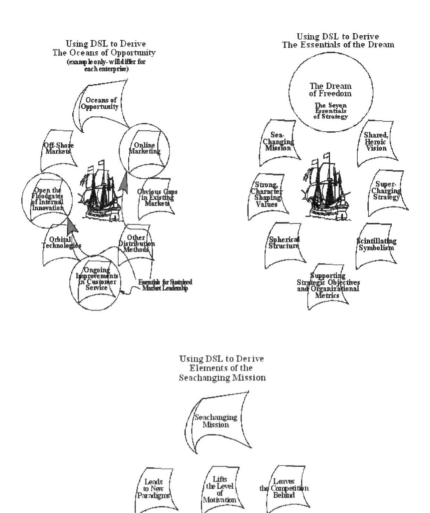

Using DSL to Derive
The Oceans of Opportunity
(example only- will differ for
each enterprise)

Oceans of
Opportunity

Off-Shore
Markets

Online
Marketing

Open the
Floodgates
of Internal
Innovation

Obvious Gaps
in Existing
Markets

Orbital
Technologies

Other
Distribution
Methods

Ongoing
Improvements
in Customer
Service

Essentials for Sustained
Market Leadership

Using DSL to Derive
The Essentials of the Dream

The Dream
of Freedom

The Seven
Essentials
of Strategy

Sea-
Changing
Mission

Shared,
Heroic
Vision

Strong,
Character
Shaping
Values

Super-
Charging
Strategy

Spherical
Structure

Scintillating
Symbolism

Supporting
Strategic Objectives
and Organizational
Metrics

Using DSL to Derive
Elements of the
Seachanging Mission

Seachanging
Mission

Leads
to New
Paradigms

Lifts
the Level
of
Motivation

Leaves
the Competition
Behind

APPENDIX II
Knowledge-Work Measurement

Replacing the Annual Appraisal

Until now, management control has been based primarily on the classic, mechanistic model: the negative feedback loop. This control system, which works wonderfully for machinery, depends on measuring variations (negative feedback) from a set point and applying external control to bring the system back into alignment with the set point. The annual performance appraisal has been the primary measurement system in the knowledge-work environment.

The problem with this system in the workplace is that the feedback is so infrequent and the standards so unclear that wide divergence from the desired performance often occurs, requiring negative feedback to attempt to bring performance back in line with the organization's goals. And while people need some negative feedback to stay in touch with reality, high performance from knowledge workers requires constant positive reinforcement based on measured performance against standards of excellence.

Feedback received from the annual performance appraisal is almost never accurate and usually serves only to point out how far the boss's and the employee's perceptions have diverged since the last appraisal. And since all work is a process and no process can be in control without real-time feedback, this system can never result in a highly productive and innovative environment.

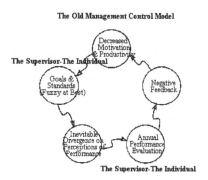

The model for the twenty-first-century knowledge-work environment is the positive feed forward model, the Developmentship Model, wherein the people have a clear understanding of the organization's mission, vision, values, and performance standards as a basis for continuous positive reinforcement in terms of the person's comparison with a standard of peak performance identified synergistically by the work team.

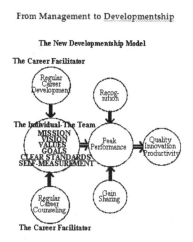

With such a system, the former manager is free to become a coach, a mentor, a Career Facilitator, or more of a support system, rather than a paternalistic boss who must periodically pass judgment on the employee.

But such a system requires process standards, which have been almost completely missing from the knowledge-work environment until now. The process standards have been missing because the key knowledge-work processes have never been defined before.

The Processes

The new paradigm is that high-quality, ever-improving customer service is the process we use to make the knowledge worker highly productive. And we know that the process necessary for making the knowledge worker high achieving is the career-development process. With the advent of new peak-performance tools and the DSL model, we can clearly measure, document, and continuously improve these processes.

More precisely, we can define the processes and allow people to self-measure their adherence to process standards. And for the first time, people can generate their own constant, accurate, and valid feedback on their performance so that they can consistently improve and become highly productive and fully achieving. It has been known that if you can get processes right and keep improving them, the desired results or outcomes of the processes are automatic. But there is another important aspect of the new paradigm.

We now know that customer satisfaction does not automatically improve simply by periodically surveying the customer and providing the workers with this feedback. We know that there is a limit to how often we can survey customers without their tiring of it and wondering why we do not respond to the feedback they have already given us several times.

Competitive Leadership Requires that People Be Number One

"Jack Welch remarked that 'the idea of liberation and empowerment for our work force is not enlightenment—it's a competitive necessity.'"
—Tom Perry, *Offensive Strategy*, Lee p. 158

"A well-run company relies heavily on individual or group initiatives for innovation and creative energy. The individual employee is utilized to the fullest extent of his creative and productive capacity."

"Treating people—not money, machines, or minds—as the natural resource may be the key to it all."
—Kenichi Ohmae, head of McKinsey's Tokyo Office, *In Search of Excellence*, p. 39

"Kimsey Mann, the chief executive of Blue Bell, the world's second-largest apparel maker, referring the eight attributes of management excellence on which this book is based, asserts that 'every one of the eight is about people.'"
—*In Search of Excellence*, p. 39

Without even surveying the customer, we know that greater teamwork focused on improving service quality will almost always result in better customer service. And we should be anticipating new ways to serve customers that the customers have not yet even discovered they need. How is teamwork in the office, which everyone knows is imperative to high performance, elicited?

The answer is to clearly define the service-delivery and career-development processes, establish process standards, and enable the owners of the processes to constantly survey themselves and continually improve these processes so they consistently meet the established standards of excellence. We know the real key to staying competitive is to tap into the synergy of teams throughout the organization by using new tools, such as the DSL model.

The process measures must help bring about this teamwork, which has long been missing from the office workplace; they must make the team highly innovative by eliciting all of their creative potential. Never before have knowledge processes been defined. They have always been underperforming. But with today's job crisis in America, they must now be brought under control and maximized.

And we must, with new organizational science, rise to a level of peak performance at the front line and at all other orbits of the organization.

Process Measures

Our new Career Facilitator must provide the tools people need to be able to do highly productive work and the information they need to measure and control themselves. Any other approach renders the data collection effort too complex and too inherently problematic to be sustained over time. Fortunately, the performance paradox and the advent of process measures make possible the establishment of process self-control in the knowledge-work environment.

We know that knowledge-worker productivity is contingent upon optimizing the customer-service process and that the knowledge worker's achievement of his or her full creative potential is dependent upon a diligently pursued career-development process. If we get the measures right, establish standards of excellence, and begin to measure these processes on a real-time basis, the desired outcomes—customer satisfaction and high performance at a competitive cost—will come naturally.

**Moving from Measuring Results Only
to Also Measuring Knowledge Work Processes**

To MANAGE, we must Control
To CONTROL, we must Measure
To MEASURE, we must Define
To DEFINE, we must Quantify.

To DEVELOP, we must provide for Self-Control
To PROVIDE FOR SELF-CONTROL, we must Em-
power people TO MEASURE THEIR OWN
PERFORMANCE
To PROVIDE FOR SELF-MEASUREMENT, we must
Define the CAREER DEVELOPMENT and
CUSTOMER SERVICE processes

Herein lies the difficulty with all previous attempts to measure knowledge-worker performance (and this writer tried scores of unsuccessful approaches before discovering the performance paradox). What *are* valid process measures, how is the data collected, what are the right process standards, and how is the data graphically displayed so that it can be acted upon to constantly improve the processes?

We have long known that no one understands the work to be done as well as the person doing that work. So, obviously, the place to start in formulating an effective process control system for our new career developer is with teams of people doing similar work. The question the team must answer in identifying the process elements for career development is: "What set of activities, performed on a weekly basis, will result in the maximization of my career potential in the most expeditious manner?" Why weekly? For office and knowledge work, weekly is real-time. While measurement can and will occur on a daily basis, the knowledge worker must have the freedom to operate the two processes with appropriate urgency, but not inordinate pressure. Monthly process measurement for the knowledge worker represents too little urgency and will result in a loss of focus on the processes. Once these activities have been identified, it is easy to develop the weekly career-development survey instrument. The team can then decide what level of performance constitutes excellence, which becomes the process standard.

The measurement instrument for service quality is developed in a similar fashion. The question to be answered by the team is: "What activities do we as a team and as individuals need to engage in weekly in order to continually improve the quality and cost effectiveness of service from this organization?" Again, the team decides what levels of performance constitute excellence and peak performance and establishes peak performance as the goal of performance for individuals and teams.

The above approach of course, is a generic one. And while it has value, it is entirely possible and desirable to develop very job-specific behavioral standards of performance. Every job has a set of behaviors that will yield peak performance and can be readily identified by teams of people doing similar work.

Measuring Knowledge-Worker Process Performance

- Teams of similar types of workers collaboratively define the behavioral aspects of their jobs in terms of accelerated career development and legendary customer service.
- The team constructs a weekly self-survey that quantifies their performance.
- The team agrees on a score for excellent performance and a score for peak performance.
- Individual team members score themselves weekly and post their scores graphically outside their workspace and on the Local Area Network.
- The team scorekeeper averages the scores and posts both comparative and team scores in a common area and on the computer network.
- The Career Facilitator interviews individual team members and identifies specific actions that resulted in each team member's score.
- The team meets monthly, reviews the standards, and upgrades them as necessary to improve their effectiveness.

Some may question the validity of defining knowledge work in terms of behaviors. America's knowledge workers admit to consistently wasting almost forty percent of their time under today's largely undefined knowledge work processes (see numerous studies on this reality on the World Wide Web), but will at first no doubt question the need to behaviorally define their work processes (they cannot favorably be defined quantitatively),

The fact remains, however, that any process without definition and near real-time measurement and feedback is out of control and underperforming. And because it is impossible to usefully define knowledge work quantitatively, it must of necessity be defined behaviorally. The key to finally submitting knowledge work to behavioral standards is to allow the work team to establish its own standards and to seek to continue to drive the process to perfection as manufacturing workers did in revolutionizing manufacturing productivity and quality in the '70s and '80s.

Some may also question the validity of the principles of self-measurement. Won't people fudge and cheat and lie about their performance, especially if pay, promotions, and recognition might be affected by the self-generated scores? No, because the Career Facilitator will validate the scores during the monthly career counseling and performance session with the worker. And besides that, peer review will quickly correct any serious falsification of the measures by individuals. Even more importantly, most people are basically honest and want valid, real-time feedback on performance. As far as the standards go, it has been shown repeatedly that people, if allowed to set their own standards, will consistently set higher standards for themselves than those above them would have.

The measurement process itself, which has always been a major obstacle to measuring people processes, involves another paradox that for the first time makes the concept of real-time and valid process measurement possible for the knowledge worker. This paradox is that the process performance data lies entirely within the person in the knowledge-work environment—not within outputs or outcomes. The person no longer has to undergo the complexity and difficulty of obtaining external data on process performance. Since he or she is the product, and since the customer-service process is also entirely behavioral, it follows that all the data on the process lies within the person. Process measurement becomes a simple and developmental exercise in surveying one's own performance on an ongoing basis throughout the week, or at a minimum, once a week.

Quantifying process performance involves scoring and charting one's performance on a weekly basis. And equally important to the success of this new method of measuring performance is that the person is entirely in control and fully capable of meeting or exceeding the performance standards.

With this paradigm, all the obstacles that have so long hindered process control of knowledge work are gone. And we validate these processes on an ongoing basis with the outcomes of customer satisfaction, revenue generation, profitability, market leadership, price leadership, etc. As with all processes, these processes can only be fully understood with ongoing trial and error and must be continually improved. Of course, the measures will change as people grow and become increasingly more expert at using new service-quality technologies and career-development strategies.

Measuring the Career-Development Process

Sample Career-Development Standards—Programmer

1. I have a career-planning document with established skills development milestones.

1   2   3   4   5

2. This week I spent at least two hours in off-site study of programming techniques and principles.

1   2   3   4   5

3. This week I explored and/or experimented with new technologies relating to my specific programming area.

1   2   3   4   5

4. This week I added one or more names to my career network and connected with them via social or professional networks.

1   2   3   4   5

5. I have identified an underdeveloped area of expertise in my career field and have spent time seeking to advance the state of the art in this area.

1   2   3   4   5

6. This week I achieved scheduled milestones on my job projects and updated my Career Facilitator on my project progress.

1   2   3   4   5

7. This week I spent at least an hour of quality time with my career and skills mentors.

1   2   3   4   5

8. This week I read trade journals in my career field, *Business Week*, and *Fortune*, and reviewed international business news related to my industry.

1   2   3   4   5

Measuring the Customer-Service Process

Sample Customer-Service Standards—Programmer

1. This week I met with my primary customer(s), seeking an in-depth understanding of their expectations of my outcomes.
1   2   3   4   5

2. This week I reviewed project progress with my primary customer and revised the project schedule as needed.
2   3   4   5

3. This week I sought peer review of my work and improved my programming quality by implementing his or her suggestions.
1   2   3   4   5

4. This week I did in-depth research to increase my programming quality.
1   2   3   4   5

5. This week I synergized with my associates either face-to-face or online, seeking new ideas on how to improve the programming work process.
1   2   3   4   5

6. This week I tracked my programming errors and reduced the number of errors significantly from the previous week.
1   2   3   4   5

7. This week I tracked my lines of error-free code written and compared this number with my goal for personal efficiency.
1   2   3   4   5

Graphical Feedback on Knowledge Work Performance

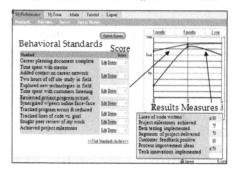

APPENDIX III
Economic Value Added

Achieving Peak Performance

With goals established and the initiation of self-measurement of the career-development and customer-service processes, using the weekly self-survey instruments and the graph illustrated in chapter 12, people now have the power to achieve peak performance in the knowledge-work and office environment.

Having laid the groundwork for peak performance, how do people convert this performance into compensation based on individual contribution to the bottom line?

Economic Value Added

We know that, generally, people have the capacity to add value to the organization in direct proportion to their salaries. In other words, a person's salary is a fairly accurate assessment of that person's expected minimum revenue contribution to the organization. Of course, in actuality, we know that the value of individuals to an organization varies widely and is often far out of proportion to their salaries.

The factors that determine the person's *actual* contribution to the revenues are one's innovativeness (by actualizing one's creative potential), one's effectiveness in improving the organization's productive capacity (by achieving job goals), and the level of day-to-day service quality the person delivers.

Having learned how to define, quantify, and measure the processes that make a person innovative, effective, and service-driven (with the career-development and customer-service process measures), it is possible to calculate the actual economic value of a knowledge worker to an organization. The formula for calculating individual economic value added in terms of bottom-line revenue is:

$$\text{Total Revenues} \times \frac{\text{Individual Salary}}{\text{Total Salaries}} \times \frac{\text{Ave. Ind. Process Score}}{\text{Standard of Excellence}} = \text{EVA}$$

Thus, with knowledge of personnel costs and revenues, it becomes possible to determine one's actual contribution to revenue generation as often as this information can be provided. Since the measured processes address not only the achievement of job goals, but the *how*, or the *process* of this achievement, the economic value added is not only quantitatively accurate—it is quality enhancing and developmental as well.

This approach assumes, of course, that teams have, with the assistance of their Career Facilitator, arrived at realistic excellence and peak-performance scores for the career-development and customer-service processes and are tracking and recording these scores. And, of course, this same methodology can and should be used to calculate team contributions to the bottom line so that tying pay to performance can be used to motivate both teams and individuals.

The Full Integration of Individual and Corporate Needs and Goals

With economic value added and the peak-performance process, it is possible, for the first time, to fully integrate individual and corporate goals and to begin to develop the true productive capacity of the office workforce. It is now possible to maximize the growth of people and to arrive at a person's true economic value to the organization. It is now possible and imperative that we replace the annual performance appraisal with an approach that is fully in harmony with the developmental needs of people and the dynamic needs of business organizations.

The annual appraisal must now be replaced with monthly meetings with people to review their progress toward their career and job goals and for mentoring them and facilitating their growth and development. Raises, bonuses, and promotions can now be based on person's economic value to the organization—and not on a subjective appraisal process.

Having given people the tools of peak performance and the motivation that comes from focusing on their growth and development, we are going to finally see a *revolution* in office productivity and quality.

A Challenge to the Leadership

The true potential of the knowledge worker has not yet been discovered. It is the challenge of corporate leadership to set out from the Old World of Management on a voyage to discover the New World of Developmentship.

What are the keys to discovery? They are the same as they were for Christopher Columbus—vision, courage, idealism, and navigational skill. What was Columbus's secret to navigating his way to the New World? It was *real-time feedback* on the navigational process.

Unlike any other navigator of his day, Columbus required his pilots to generate *constant* feedback on direction and frequent measurement of the speed of his ship. He had a slate hung near the wheel and compass; every fifteen minutes, the pilot was required to accurately identify the ship's direction and record it on the slate so that the desired heading could be maintained accurately.

By this method, and his extensive knowledge of the known world, Columbus became history's greatest dead-reckoning navigator. His plan was to sail due west from the Canary Islands until he reached what he thought would be India. From years of research and experience, he knew of the circular trade winds that would both take him and bring him back from his remote destination. Thirty-three days after departing, he and his band arrived at the New World that was to become America.

What are the lessons for corporate leadership? First, it is not known what is beyond the borders of the Old World of Management. But it is known that something wonderful exists with the potential of the knowledge worker. Secondly, it is known that real-time feedback on the two processes of *career development* and *customer service* is required to make this journey.

So, the challenge for corporate leadership is to recognize that its primary customer is the people of the organization, to collaboratively define the process of serving this customer, and then to spend most of its time focusing on maximizing its people's career development and ability to satisfy their customers. This kind of focus will inevitably yield far greater financial results for the organization than the paper entrepreneurship that seems to preoccupy so many top executives today. It bears repeating that Citibank's Walter Wriston said, "The person that learns how to harness the genius of his or her own people, will blow away the competition."

With this example, the leader can challenge his or her people to define their work process and to begin to generate real-time, graphical feedback on these processes. Only then can the true performance of the knowledge worker be realized.

A Challenge to the Knowledge Worker

The full potential of the individual has not yet been discovered. One man came very close to achieving his full productive potential. Benjamin Franklin made major contributions to almost every field of human endeavor and spent a lifetime helping bring about the birth of the free and prosperous new nation of America.

What was Benjamin Franklin's's secret for high achievement? It was real-time feedback on character development. Someone long ago said, "Sow a thought, reap an action, sow an action, reap a habit, sow a habit, reap a character, sow a character, and reap a destiny." On the ship back from England at the age of twenty-one, after having dissipated somewhat, he established the life goal to make his maximum contribution to bringing the dream of freedom and prosperity to life by establishing the only written goal of his life: "achieve moral perfection."

After arriving back in Philadelphia, he identified thirteen universal success principles and defined his values with reference to these principles. He then designed his time-management system and a system of daily self-evaluation with graphical feedback, his real-time feedback system on personal performance. In his old age, he recorded in his autobiography his belief that this system was largely responsible for his success and happiness in life.

What are the lessons for the knowledge worker? First of all, the lesson is that the wellspring of achievement is *character* and that the life goal must be to achieve congruence with universal principles and one's governing values based on these principles. Secondly, it must be learned that the principle of real-time feedback on process performance is essential to peak performance in the workplace.

Every individual must recognize his or her mission to achieve his or her full potential for service. The two processes that must be measured on a real-time basis are the career-development and customer-service processes.

The challenge then to every knowledge worker is to begin to strive for congruence with universal principles and personal values based on these principles and to discover, develop, and give his or her special and unique gift to the world using the peak-performance process.

APPENDIX IV
Enterprise Developer

The Chrysalis Leadership Experience is the synergistic recasting by the leadership team and representatives from the ranks of the overall strategy of the organization in terms of society's highest values, using the DSL model. All seven essentials of strategy must be developed. This strategic thinking is the number-one job of the leadership team. People are incredibly motivated by a powerful organizational vision that is in harmony with America's purpose and founding values. Such a vision, clearly and constantly communicated to all orbits of the organization, elicits uncommon loyalty, dedication, and innovation from people.

This exercise should be conducted over a period of a few weeks, preferably offsite, so that there is total focus on the derivation of the organization's strategy. It must embed the leadership's passion, commitment, and dedication to bringing the dreams of its people to life. Chester I. Barnard, legendary CEO of New Jersey Bell for twenty-five years and, later, Harvard business professor, taught that a true leader's job is to maximize the growth opportunities of their people and to help them achieve their full career portential.

This kind of deep commitment to people, their dreams of freedom,

219

to the founding purpose of America, to leading them to a higher standard of performance, and to the full extent of their career potential is a supercharging leadership strategy. But more importantly, it is the fundamental purpose of leadership. It is the most important factor in ultimately maximizing stakeholder value. Great truths are almost always paradoxical and focusing on people's growth and development rather than on maximizing stock price, quarterly earnings, and other measures of organizational success is simply the best strategy for maximizing the organization's service and financial potential.

Once the seven essentials of strategy are fully defined, the leadership's main job is to travel to every orbit of the organization and to communicate it with evangelistic fervor on a sustained basis to the organization's people. When the organization's people fully catch the ennobling vision of the leadership—that they and their dreams are the product—they will proceed toward the accomplishment of the organization's quantitative goals (the strategic objectives) with unheard of diligence and dedication. They are eager and amazingly adept at maximizing the organization's measures of success (revenues, market share, quarterly earnings, etc.) when given a structure of synergy, gainsharing, profit sharing, stock ownership, and real-time feedback on the financial measures.

The more the organization can cause people to experience the concept of individual free enterprise within the workplace, the more creative, innovative, and productive that individual will be. With the potential to calculate individual and team economic value added to the organization, a model for continuous organizational improvement, and an ennobling mission and vision, there is the real possibility of moving to a new plateau of performance and bringing our jobs back home. Because, with these conditions, the leadership has reached the wellspring of American genius, the possibility again for people to truly achieve the American Dream.

Once the leadership has defined the strategy in terms of building America and the dream of freedom worldwide and, in the process, experienced a personal metamorphosis in their leadership paradigm, the people must be empowered to transform the organization and to improve it on a continuous basis. A new tool that has emerged for this job is called *Enterprise Developer*. Enterprise Developer uses collaborative LAN networks and the Internet to elicit the creative potential of people at all levels and orbits of the organization using the Seven Determinants and the DSL models as a structure for synergy. Following are a description of and a number of examples of this process.

The Continuous Organization Development Process

- The leadership dedicates itself primarily to strategy formulation, constantly sharpening the strategic vision using the seven essentials of dynamic number one, *the dream of freedom,* and generating the right metrics.
- Team members identify the dynamic or determinant that they have primary influence in, such as, for example, *drive to market or oceans of opportunity.*
- Team members meet weekly or use collaborative, online applications to synergize in identifying, for example, the seven essentials of the marketing dynamic, using the DSL model.
- Once the seven essentials for a specific organization are identified, teams synergize to derive the seven elements of each of the essentials, using the DSL model.
- Teams identify action items for each essential and element.
- Action items are prioritized for maximum effect.
- Assignments are made for each of the action items.

Seven Determinants of Global Competitiveness for Universal Motors Corporation

Determinant No. 1—The Dynamics of Developmentship
(The Disciplines of Business)
Dynamic (Discipline) No. 1: The Dream of Freedom
The Seven Essentials of the Dream (the Strategy) of the
Business—Showing Three Elements (*l*s) of each Essential

Essential No. 1
*Sea-changing mission: The mission must **look** to bringing the dream of freedom to life, **lead** to entirely new business, and **link** all of the organization's efforts to the development of the full career potential of its people.*

Example: *Freedom at work*

Essential No. 2

*Shared, heroic goal (the vision): Our vision must **lift** the organization to new frontiers, **link** all organizational goals together, and **liberate** people to make their maximum contribution.*

Example: *Return Universal Motors to world leadership in the transportation industry by the end of this decade.*

Essential No. 3

*Strong, ennobling values: Our values must **lead** to deeper personal integrity, **lessen** the need for detailed and limiting policy manuals, and **lift** the level of service to our customers*

Example: *Our people are our primary product. We use the world's best products and customer service as tools with which to build people.*

- *Working at Universal Motors is fun.*
- *We exercise the highest integrity in everything we do.*
- *We are a highly innovative company. We lead the way in discovering new frontiers of progress in transportation.*

Essential No. 4

*Supercharging strategy: The strategy must **light** the fires of innovation and motivation, it must **let** people have the opportunity to make their maximum contribution to success, and it must **lead** to entirely new solutions for the organization's customers.*

Example: *Utilize the full potential of our people in reinventing the transportation industry and become known as one of Fortune's 100 best places in the world to work.*

Essential No. 5

*Spherical, synergistic, globally competitive business structure: The organization must **lead** its industry in innovativeness, **let** the business units be appropriately autonomous, and stay **laser** focused on its core competencies in order to maintain competitive leadership in the face of volatile, global markets.*

Example:

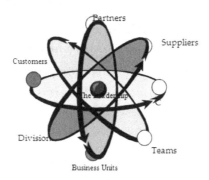

Example: UNIVERSAL MOTORS CORPORATON

Essential No. 6

Scintillating symbolism: *The corporate symbolism must* **live**, *in that it must appeal to the deepest and noblest aspirations of the organization's people and all of its stakeholders. It must* **legendarily** *state the definition of the business in seven words or less. And it must* **lyrically** *convey the meaning of the organization via a corporate song or jingle.*

Example (slogan): *Freedom at Work*

Example (corporate song): *El Capitan*

Essential No. 7

Supporting strategic objectives: *They must* **synchronize** *with the strategy,* **stretch** *the organization's performance, and* **stimulate** *innovation.*

Example: *Strategic objectives: 1) Introduce a competitive fuel-cell car by mid-2015; 2) achieve an average mileage rating of thirty-eight for all corporate vehicles by the end of 2016; 3) achieve a number-one J. D. Power rating for customer service by the end of 2013.*

*Organizational metrics: They must **look** at a balance of measures, soft and hard; they must **link** performance to the mission, vision, and values of the organization; and they must **lead** to continuous innovation from the organization's people and business units.*

Example: Organizational metrics: *Customer satisfaction indices, people satisfaction, amount of revenue generated annually by new products, earnings, cash flow, productivity, capital turnover, people turnover, and career development of the people.*

Dynamic (Discipline) No. 2: Debt-Minimizing Capitalization
The Seven Essentials of Debt-Minimizing Capitalization

Essential No. 1

Example: *Solidly invested savings from earnings* (at least three elements all starting with the letter *L*)

Essential No. 2

Example: *Sold-out stock issues* (at least three elements all starting with the letter *L*)

Essential No. 3

Example: *Studied use of leverage* (at least three elements all starting with the letter *L*)

Essentials No. 4-7: (Create for your organization—must start with an *S*); (at least three elements all starting with the letter *L*)

Examples: *Sale of unneeded assets, subsidies in the form of government grants, sales-tax breaks from local government, swift recovery of past-due accounts receivable, etc.*

Dynamic No. 3: Developmental Marketing
The Seven Essentials of Developmental Marketing

Essential No. 1

Example: *Segmentation of markets into those in which leadership can be achieved* (at least three elements all starting with the letter *L*)

Essential No. 2

Example: *Selection of niches that can generate high margins* (at least three elements all starting with the letter *L*)

Essential No. 3

Example: *Systematic customer surveys and studied market research* (at least three elements all starting with the letter *L*)

Essential No. 4

Example: *State-of-the-art marketing channels* (at least three elements all starting with the letter *L*)

Essential No. 5

Example: *Sales forces that are solutions-oriented and close to the customers* (at least three elements all starting with the letter *L*)

Essential No. 6

Example: (Identify for your company—must start with the letter *S*); (at least three elements all starting with the letter *L*)

Essential No. 7 (Identify for your company—must start with the letter *S*); (at least three elements all starting with the letter *L*)

Dynamic (Discipline) No. 4: The Discipline of Quality
The Seven Essentials

Essential No. 1

Example: *Self-generation of real-time process measures in the production processes* (at least three elements all starting with the letter *L*)

Essential No. 2

Example: *Systematic customer feedback, surveys, and focus groups* (at least three elements all starting with the letter *L*)

Essential No. 3

Example: *Strict product specifications* (at least three elements all starting with the letter *L*)

Essential No. 4

Example: *Strong supplier relationships and standards* (at least three elements all starting with the letter *L*)

Essential No. 5

Example: *Scheduled activity on the part of teams to improve process performance* (at least three elements all starting with the letter *L*)

Essential No. 6

Example: *Studies of the product's environmental compatibility by independent testing laboratories* (at least three elements all starting with the letter *L*)

Essential No. 7

Example: *Stringent and continuous testing of the products and services* (at least three elements all starting with the letter *L*)

**Dynamic (Discipline No. 5): The Diligence of Financial Control
The Seven Essentials**

Essential No. 1

Example: *Strict adherence to appropriate debt to equity ratios* (at least three elements all starting with the letter *L*)

Essential No. 2

Example: *Synergistic cost containment with gainsharing for cost containment participants* (at least three elements all starting with the letter *L*)

Essential No. 3

Example: *Synchronization of growth rate with ability to maintain product- and service-quality standards* (at least three elements all starting with the letter *L*)

Essential No. 4

Example: *Sustained stock price through limits on equity issues and/or stock buybacks* (at least three elements all starting with the letter *L*)

Essential No. 5

Example: *Studied and wise executive compensation tied to balanced and improving, long-term financial performance* (at least three elements all starting with the letter *L*)

Essential No. 6

Example: *Sharing of earnings with all stakeholders including the organization's people* (at least three elements all starting with the letter *L*)

Essential No. 7

Example: *Systematic shedding of nonperforming products and businesses* (at least three elements all starting with the letter *L*)

Dynamic (Discipline) No. 6: The Daring to Innovate
The Seven Essentials of Innovation

Essential No. 1

Example: *Seek to recreate, reinvent, and redefine the industry* (at least three elements all starting with the letter *L*).

Essential No. 2

Example: *Synergize at all levels, systematically and with structure* (at least three elements all starting with the letter *L*).

Essential No. 3

Example: *Stipulate that for all business units and product teams, at least 25 percent of annual revenues must be from new products and services* (at least three elements all starting with the letter *L*).

Essential No. 4

Example: *Seek to spin off competitors from within—capitalize great business ideas generated by the organization's people* (at least three elements all starting with the letter *L*).

Essential No. 5

Example: *Set up skunk works independent from the main business units for pioneering new products* (at least three elements all starting with the letter *L*).

Essential No. 6

Example: *Structure executive teams to systematically listen, study, and screen new product ideas by the organization's people* (at least three elements all starting with the letter *L*).

Essential No. 7

Example: *Share gains from innovations with the creators of the innovations* (at least three elements all starting with the letter *L*).

Dynamic (Discipline) No. 7: The Dedication to Developmentship
The Seven Essentials

Essential No. 1

Example: *Seize the great opportunities in diversity in the workplace* (at least three elements all starting with the letter *L*).

Essential No. 2

Example: *Sincerely love the people more than profits* (at least three elements all starting with the letter *L*).

Essential No. 3

Example: *Systematically and continually recognize excellence* (at least three elements all starting with the letter *L*).

Essential No. 4

Example: *Spend more time in the field listening to people and less time in the office solving operating problems—delegate the solutions* (at least three elements all starting with the letter *L*).

Essential No. 5

Example: *Stop merging and acquiring and start developing the enormous creative potential of the existing organization* (at least three elements all starting with the letter *L*).

Essential No. 6

Example: *See my job as learning how to use service as a means of developing people rather than using people to deliver service* (at least three elements all starting with the letter *L*).

Essential No. 7

Example: *Share gains and earnings at all levels of the organization* (at least three elements all starting with the letter *L*).

Determinant No. 2: Oceans of Opportunity
Dynamic (Discipline) No. 1: Online Marketing
The Seven Essentials

Examples: *State of the arttate-of-the-art website; Superior customer service; Sensible warranties and return policies; Simple ordering process; Sufficient feedback on order status; Specialized, automated picking and packing; Synchronization of supply with demand through intelligent forecasting—at least three "elements" should be derived for each of these essentials.*

Dynamics 2–7: Examples: *Offshore markets, Orbital technologies, Ongoing improvements in customer service, Obvious gaps in existing markets, Other distribution methods, Opening of the floodgates of innovation of the organization's people*

Determinant No. 3: Seas of Competition
Dynamic No. 1: Systematic Price Cutting by Competitors
The Seven Essentials

Examples: *Steady price enhancement through cost reduction; Savings on warranty claims through consistent quality improvements; Substitution of low-margin products with high-margin innovations; Systematic introduction of new styles; Stressing of product uniqueness; Sustained improvements in customer service; Seeking out constantly new, untapped market segments and niches—at least three "elements" should be derived for each of these essentials.*

Dynamics (Disciplines) 2–7

Examples: *Systematic dumping by offshore competitors; Sudden obsolescence of entire product lines by technological advances; Steady dilution of proprietary technologies through imitations; Suits by competitors for alleged patent infringements; Sustained deregulation, resulting in a constant flow of new competitors; Stealing of intellectual capital by recruiters; Sea changes in societal norms brought on by the Internet, other new technologies, and evolutionary changes in market demographics*

Determinant No. 4: Realms of Adversity
Dynamic No. 1: Rampant Departure of Key People
in Times of Rapid Economic Expansion
The Seven Essentials

Essentials: Examples—*Strong incentives for in-house people to upgrade knowledge and skills; Superior cafeteria of benefits; Staying above industry average on wages; Showing intense interest in the career development of people; Showering people with appreciation; Sharing profits and gains; Seeing that the workplace is fun, fulfilling, and conducive to family life—at least three "elements" should be derived for each of these essentials.*

Essentials 2–7: Examples—*Radical increases in the cost of capital; Rising costs of raw materials; Repeated tightening of environmental-impact standards; Recurring shortages in raw materials; Ravaging weather phenomena; Real, long-term shortages of high-tech workers; Resistance to market entry by offshore economies*

Determinant No. 5: Environments of Concern
Dynamic No. 1: Ecosystem Impact Awareness and Priority
The Seven Essentials

Essentials: Examples—*Stressing of reverence for the environment by the leadership at every opportunity, Strong recycling program, Sensitivity to input by environmental groups, Serious effort to reduce waste at every point in the organization, Surrounding of the facilities with the beauty of nature, Subduing of noise pollution at all locations, Strict adherence to existing environmental regulations—at least three "elements" should be derived for each of these essentials.*

Dynamics 2-7: Examples—*Environmental-impact studies for all growth initiatives, Erring on the side of conservation, Evaluation of each product and service for environmental compatibility, Energy-conservation methods exhaustively applied, Education of the organization continuously on environmental matters, Emulation of industry leaders in environmental compliance and enhancement*

Determinant No. 6: Winds of Change
Dynamic No. 1: Worldwide Technological
Advances in Every Field of Endeavor
The Seven Essentials

Essentials: Examples—*Sea changes in distribution channels, Steadily advancing information systems technologies, Synergistic relationships with suppliers, Strong alliances with service providers, Studied use of outsourcing, State-of-the-art communications technologies, Soft technology advances (such as personal effectiveness training and tools)—at least three "elements" should be derived for each of these essentials.*

Dynamics 2–7: Examples—*Third-world imperatives, Torrential flow of information, The aging population, Total equalization of pay for equal work, Transformation of the knowledge-work environment with new paradigms of performance, Trend toward holistic quality of life considerations by all people, Tremendous availability of senior-age peoples for part- and full-time opportunities*

Determinant No. 7: Anchors of Survival
Dynamic No. 1: Example—Adherence to
the Corporate Governing Values
The Seven Essentials

Essentials: Examples—*Symbolize the values at the top; Stress the values at every opportunity; Solidify the values through business stories; Specialize the day planners to include the values; See the values as the main control system of the organization; Share the values through written, verbal, and nonverbal communication constantly—at least three "elements" should be derived for each of these essentials.*

Dynamics 2–7: Examples—*Avoidance of excess debt-to-equity ratios, Application of conservative accounting practices, Aggressive cost-containment strategies, Abandonment of nonperforming assets, Acquisitions and mergers based on their potential to provide increased opportunities for people, Achievement of harmony with the environment and the community*

APPENDIX V
Continuous Organization Development
- A Review & Variants

1. Enterprise Developer is designed to serve as a *structure for synergy* in the comprehensive, holistic, and continuous improvement of organizational effectiveness over an extended period of time. Individuals and teams should select *one* determinant and *one* dynamic to work on at a time.

2. After selecting one of the determinants of global competitiveness, the first dynamic of that determinant should be derived using the alliteration methodology illustrated in the examples. The dynamics all start with the letter *D* for the disciplines of business, called in this work, *The Dynamics of Developmentship.*

3. The dynamics of the other determinants are derived by utilizing the first letter of the determinant. For example, the seven dynamics of the *Oceans of Opportunity* start with the letter *O.* It is important to stick with this methodology in using the model. Alliteration is a *derivational* principle in the model.

4. Upon identifying a dynamic of a determinant, the seven essentials of that dynamic should then be derived.

5. Upon completing the derivation of the seven essentials of a dynamic, three elements should be derived for each of the seven essentials.

6. From the derived elements or essentials, a list of action items for improvement should be formulated and prioritized.

7. After prioritizing the list of needed improvement actions, responsibility for implementation and a target date should be identified for each action.

8. As with anything worthwhile, effective use of Enterprise Developer is hard work. The initial inclination will be to quickly abandon the alliteration methodology and revert to traditional freewheeling brainstorming. This inclination must be resisted. The model works extremely well. Use of it becomes increasingly easy and fun after exercising the required effort to develop skill in the derivational method.

9. After using the discipline of alliteration in the derivation of the essentials of organizational effectiveness using the proscribed *S*s for the essentials and the *L*s for the elements, other letters can and should be experimented with in the derivations.

10. If the decision to use derivational letters for an organizational dynamic's essentials and elements other than *S*s and *l*s, is made, such as, for example, the letter *M* for Market segmentation for leadership in the industry, all of the essentials should then be derived using the letter *M*. The elements might then, for example, be called "Niches" and all start with the letter *N*. Any and all letters can work, but the alliteration method is critical in the use of the model.

11. While all business units, divisions, departments, sections, and work teams, are governed by the *seven determinants,* the six determinants other than the *Dynamics of Developmentship,* are best addressed by the leadership of the organization. Improvement of organizational effectiveness by smaller organizational units can be best carried on by a comprehensive treatment of the *Dynamics of Developmentship.*

12. For example, the dynamic, *The Discipline of Quality,* should be the main focus of those in the organization responsible for production, service, and quality control. Enterprise Developer makes possible a holistic, detailed, and exhaustive analysis of a business dynamic and the systematic identification and implementation of improvement strategies, eventually resulting in the achievement of *peak performance* by the work group.

13. Upon completion of the derivation of the essentials and elements for a given discipline within the organization, and the implementation of improvement strategies, the process should be repeated, the derivations revised, updated, and new improvement strategies should be identified. Continuous improvement in every facet of the enterprise is essential for maintaining competitive leadership over time as the *trade winds of change* continue to transform markets and economies.

APPENDIX VI

Using Word as a Platform for Organization Development

Collaborating with Word Only

Collaborating with the DSL process and Word only involves the team leader e-mailing a Word document with a draft of the beginning derivation to the work team and requesting feedback in the form of comments. Recipients open the document, click on Track Changes under the Review tab, then, on New Comment. After adding as many comments as desired on the beginning derivation, the team members e-mail the document back to the team leader. The team leader clicks on Track Changes and adds his or her new comments and e-mails the document back. Having completed the collaboration, the team leader clicks Accept All Changes and e-mails the final document to all team members.

In deriving the essentials of the Discipline of Quality for a given organizational unit, for example, adjectives such as "stringent" or "strict" might be used, which would result in essentials such as "Stringent Quality Standards" and "Strict Quality Audits." At least three essentials should be identified for each of the seven disciplines.

Online collaboration will result in organizational standards that can significantly raise the level of performance by the work team.

Sharepoint 2010 Document Co-Authoring with Microsoft Word

With SharePoint, gone are the days where documents lived in a sluggish circular workflow of composition, printing, e-mailing, reviews, edits, editing approvals, and publishing. Recently, the Microsoft Office team has been narrowly focusing on making their products adhere to the cloud-based collaboration capabilities of the future.

In the case of document life-cycles for Word 2010, their solution incorporates an amazing new feature—the ability for multiple information workers to simultaneously edit and collaborate on a Word document. This process is known as *co-authoring* and happens in real-time with the seamless integration of Microsoft Office 2010 and SharePoint 2010.

Now there can be *one* document with multiple *simultaneous* authors and *real-time* editing and collaboration. No check-out/check-in is required (although it's still available), and it comes with many time-saving and productivity-boosting implications for all kinds of business operations.

Requirements:

- A SharePoint Foundation 2010 or SharePoint Server 2010 site (approximately $250/mo.)
- A document library on that site (versioning-enabled optional)
- Two or more users with contribute permissions on that document library
- Two or more users with Office 2010 installed on their client machine

How to do it:

1. Open up Microsoft Word 2010 and create a basic document with some text.
2. Save this document and upload it to your hosted SharePoint 2010 document library.
3. Have two or more users browse this library and click on the document.
4. Select Edit when this gray dialog box pops up, and then click OK.

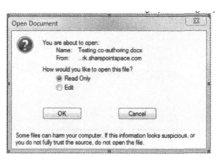

5. Enter your SharePoint 2010 credentials (check the "remember my password" checkbox).
6. Type away.

In Microsoft Word 2010:

1. At the bottom left, you should see the users who currently have the document open in Word 2010's edit mode. Click on this icon to see the usernames.
2. Have **user A** type in some text and click the Save button.
3. Now, **user B** will be alerted that updates are available.

4. When user B types in some text and clicks Save, he or she will see both content changes with a highlighted paragraph of what was just imported. After he or she saves the document again, the highlighting goes away.

5. You can also click on an author's name at the bottom left and begin a collaboration effort from within Word 2010

6. A pop-up appears when other users close Word (as seen above).

7. If you have versioning enabled in the SharePoint 2010 document library, you'll notice a new version is stored after every save.

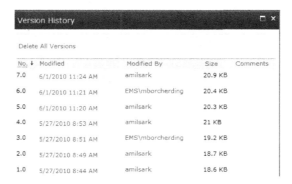

Source: Andy Milsark's Fpweb.net blog, an excellent SharePoint webhosting site (used by permission).

APPENDIX VII
Implementing Real-Time
Feedback on Performance

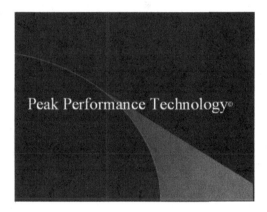

The Fundamental Premise

All work is a process. Any process without real-time measurement and feedback is *by definition* out of control

The Objective

Bring work processes under
control in order to accelerate career
growth, consistently deliver legendary customer service, and appropriately recognize and reward peak
performance

The Principles of SPC

- Clearly defined standards of performance
- Continuous self-measurement against the standards
- Real-time graphical feedback on performance
- Periodic surveys of the primary customers
- Collaborative correction of the standards based on customer satisfaction measures

The Implementation Process

- Assemble team of people with similar jobs
- Team collaboratively identifies quality parameters - *how* the job is be done
- Quality parameters include corporate values, professional disciplines, product specifications, cost effectiveness standards, customer expectations, and team protocols

DSL - Derived Solutions Logic -
A Tool for Eliciting Out-of-the
Box Thinking

- The literary device *alliteration*
- The number of completeness, *7 (at least seven standards, often more, sometimes less)*
- The principle of, *prioritization*

The Derivational Model - DSL

- Select the letter of the main function of the job such as *P,* for the job of Programmer/Analyst
- Identify the pertinent verbs and adverbs, such as *participate, plan, program, probe, present, pause, purge, prepare, post, perfect, penetratingly;* use MSWord's Thesaurus for assistance
- Create objectivity and measurability

An Example of Programmer Standards

- Participate with the customer in several in depth sessions seeking a precise understanding of the customers needs and specifications
- Plan the project, and plot project milestones on a bar chart using conservative estimates (underpromise and overdeliver), and flow chart the process
- Program an efficient algorithm, and review it with primary customer
- Probe the customer frequently for deeper insights into his needs
- Pause daily, and seek input from elite peers on quality of work
- Present graphical project feedback on progress to primary customer
- Purge the program exhaustively before beta testing
- Prepare Power Point training program on the completed program
- Perfect the Program before beta testing. Beta test.
- Pass the completed program to the customer via Power Point description
- Post operationally administer a customer survey on the quality of the product, post survey for peer and supervisory review

The Measurement Instrument

1. This week I met with the customer to clarify his precise needs.
   1   2   3   4   5
2. This I flowcharted and barcharted my project.
   1   2   3   4
3. This week I re fined and perfected my programming algorithm.
   1   2   3   4   5
4. This week I probed my customer about issues that were unclear to me.
   1   2   3   4   5
5. This week I paused to synergize with an elite peer on my quality.
   1   2   3   4   5
6. This week I presented graphical feedback on project progress to my customer.
   1   2   3   4   5
7. This week I constantly purged the program of defects.
   1   2   3   4   5
8. This week I worked on a Power Point Program with which to train and transmit.
   1   2   3   4   5

Note: To score the survey, ignore the standards that are not applicable this week.
Multiply the applicable standards by 5 for the total possible score. Divide your
total score by the total possible score for your performance index for the week.

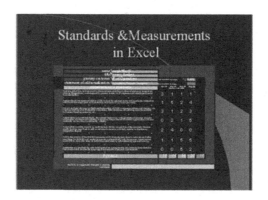

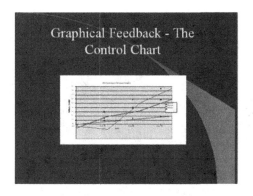

Tracking the Data

- Individual scores self weekly on Excel template, graphs and posts graph on outside of workspace for peer review
- Individual Excel performance record e-mailed to supervisor or team leader
- Supervisor or team leader consolidates team scores, charts and posts team score in common area

Validating the Standards

- Customer is resurveyed monthly
- Consolidated team customer satisfaction indexes posted in common area so that trend can be plotted
- Standards and measures revised to reflect customer feedback on quality, schedule, and cost
- Pilot group Job satisfaction survey conducted after 90 days of use of the standards

The Career Development Axiom

The most powerful things you can do for your career is to excel at your current job, and maximize personal growth in your career field.

Career Development Principles
- Integrity and interpersonal excellence
- Mastery of career speciality
- Ongoing research in career field
- Synergize with Associates, and Innovate
- Network on a continuing bases
- Broaden scope
- Mentor others

Sample Career Development Measures

1. This week I maintained a high degree of integrity in all of my dealings.

   1 2 3 4 5

2. This week I studied job related technologies and gained new mastery of my job.

   1 2 3 4 5

3. This week I did intensive research in my career field and documented my discoveries.

   1 2 3 4 5

4. This week I added and documented at least one new contact to my professional network

   and nurtured other members of my network.

   1 2 3 4 5

5. This week I collaborated with my teammates on how to streamline my job process.

   1 2 3 4 5

6. This week I read articles in *Business Week & Fortune* and monitored my company's stock price.

   1 2 3 4 5

7. This week I shared my knowledge with and mentored someone less experienced.

   1 2 3 4 5

Standards: 1-3 = Seek Career Counseling, 4-5 = Excellent, 6-7 = Peak Performance

Bibliography

Albert, Kenneth J. *The Strategic Management Handbook*. New York: McGraw-Hill, 1983.

Albrecht, Karl. *Successful Management by Objectives*. NJ: Prentice-Hall, 1978.

Allen, Louis A. *Professional Management*. New York: McGraw-Hill, 1973.

Barnard, Chester I. *The Functions of the Executive*. Harvard University Press, 1947.

Batten, J. D. *Tough Minded Management*. New York: American Management Association, 1963.

Beer, Michael. *Organization Change and Development*: A Systems View. Glenview, IL: Scott, Foresman and Company, 1980.

Benton, Lewis. *Management for the Future*. New York: McGraw-Hill, 1978.

Bessenger, R. Carlton, and W. Waino Soujanen. *Management and the Brain*. Georgia State University, 1983.

Biro, Brian D. *Beyond Success*. Montana: Pygmalion Press, 1995.

Blanchard, Kenneth, and Spencer Johnson. *The One Minute Manager*. New York: Berkley Books, 1983.

Brown, James K., "Across the Board," March 1984, p. 48.

Coonradt, Charles A., with Lee Nelson. *The Game of Work*. Orem, UT: Liberty Press, 1984.

Covey, Stephen R. *Principle-Centered Leadership,* New York: Fireside, 1990.

―――. *The 7 Habits of Highly Effective People.* New York: Fireside, 1989.

Creech, Bill. *The Five Pillars of TQM.* New York: Truman Talley Books/Dutton, 1994.

Crosby, Phillip B. *Quality Is Free,* New York: New American Library, 1979.

Deal, Terrence E., and Allan A. Kennedy. *Corporate Cultures.* California: Addison-Wesley, 1982.

Donaldson, Gordon. *Managing Corporate Wealth.* New York: Praeger, 1984.

Drucker, Peter F. *Concept of the Corporation.* New York: John Day Company, 1972.

―――. *The Effective Executive.* New York: Harper & Row, 1966.

―――. *Management, Tasks, Responsibilities, Practices.* New York: Harper & Row, 1980.

―――. *Managing in Turbulent Times.* New York: Harper & Row, 1964.

―――. *The Practice of Management.* New York: Harper & Row, 1954.

Dyer, William G. *Contemporary Issues in Management and Organizational Development.* California: Wesley Publishing Company, 1983.

Eilon, Samuel. *Management Control.* New York: Macmillan and Company, 1971.

Eliasson, Gunnar, Christopher Green, and Charles R. McCann Jr. *Microfoundations of Economic Growth*. Ann Arbor: The University of Michigan Press, 2001.

Enell, John W., and George H. Haas. *Setting Standards for Executive Performance*. American Management Association Inc., 1960.

Farand, Max, and Benjamin Franklin. *The Autobiography of Benjamin Franklin*. University of California Press, 1949.

Fayol, Henri. *General and Industrial Management*. Pitman Sons Ltd., 1949.

Fortune, September 20, 1993, 38–50.

Frankl, Victor. *Man's Search for Meaning*. New York: Pocket Books.

French, W. L., C. H. Bell Jr., and R. A. Zawacki. *Organization Development*. Plano, TX: Business Publications Inc., 1983.

Gellerman, Saul W. *Motivation and Productivity*. American Management Association Inc., 1963.

Gibson, Ivancevich, and Donnelly, *Readings in Organizations*. Business Publications Inc., 1979.

Goble, Frank G. *The Third Force*. New York: Grossman, 1970.

Guzzo, Bondy. *A Guide to Worker Productivity Experiments in the United States* 1976–1981. (New York: Pergamon Press, 1983).

Hamel, Gary and C. K. Prahalad. *Competing for the Future*. Cambridge: Harvard Business School Press, 1996.

Handy, Charles. *The Age of Unreason*. Boston: Harvard Business School Press, 1990.

Harmon, Paul. *Successful Management*. Dubuque: Kendall/Hunt Publishing Co., 1983.

Hayes, Robert H. *Restoring Our Competitive Edge: Competing through Manufacturing.* New York: John Wiley & Sons, 1984.

Hersey, Paul, and Kenneth Blanchard. *Management of Organizational Behavior.* Prentice-Hall, 1969.

Herzberg, Frederick. *Work and the Nature of Man.* New York: World Publishing, 1966.

Hickman, Craig R., and Michael A. Silva. *Creating Excellence.* New York: New American Library, 1984.

Hofstede, Geert. "The Poverty of Management Control Philosophy." *Academy of Management Review* (July 1978).

"Industry Week Magazine," June 25, 1984, p. 37–50.

Kantrow, Alan M. "Survival Strategies for American Industry." *Harvard Business Review.* John Wiley & Sons Inc., 1983.

Kappel, F. R., *Vitality in a Business Organization.* New York: McGraw-Hill, 1960.

Lee, Sang M., and Gary Schwandiman. *Japanese Management, Cultural and Environmental Consideration.* Praeger Publishers, 1982.

Lincoln, James F. *Incentive Management.* (The Lincoln Electric Company, Ohio, 1951).

Macquarrie, John. *In Search of Humanity.* New York: Crossroad, 1983.

Maddi, S. R., and P. T. Costa. *Humanism in Psychology.* New York, 1983.

Madsen, K. B. *Modern Theories of Motivation.* New York: John Wiley & Sons, 1974.

Maslow, Abraham H. *Toward a Psychology of Being.* New York: Nostrand Company Inc., 1962.

Mason, Richard O. and E. Burton Swanson. *Measurement for Management Decision.* (New Youk: Addison Wesley Publishing Co., 1981).

McEachern, William. *Managerial Control and Performance.* (New York: Lexington Books, 1975).

McGregor, D. *The Human Side of Enterprise.* New York: McGraw-Hill, 1960.

Meyers, M. Scott. *Every Employee a Manager.* McGraw-Hill, 1981.

Miles, Robert H. *MACRO Organizational Behavior.* Santa Monica: Goodyear Publishing, 1980.

Miller, Earnest C. *Objectives and Standards: An Approach to Planning and Control.* (New York American Management Association Inc. 1966).

Mockler, Robert J. *The Management Control Process.* (New York: Meredith Corporation, 1972)

Mohr, Lawrence B. *Explaining Organizational Behavior.* San Francisco: Jossey-Bass Publishers, 1982.

Naisbitt, John. *Megatrends.* New York: Warner Books, 1982.

The New York Times Magazine, September 13, 1970, 33, 122–126.

Ohmae, Keniche. *The Mind of the Strategist.* (New York, McGraw-Hill, 1982).

Osborne, David and Ted Gaebler. *Reinventing Government.* New York: Addison-Wesley, 1992.

Ouchi, William G. *Theory Z.* San Francisco, (Ca: Addison-Wesley, 1981).

Pascale, R. T., and A. G. Athos. *The Art of Japanese Management.* (New York: Warner Books, 1981).

Patchen, Martin, *Participation, Achievement, and Involvement on the Job.* New York: Prentice-Hall, 1970.

Patchin, Robert I. *The Management and Maintenance of Quality Circles.* Irwin, IL: Dow-Jones Inc., 1983.

Paula,De and Willsmore, A.W.. *The Techniques of Business Control.* (New York: 1973: Pitman Publishing))

Perry, Lee Tom. *Offensive Strategy.* New York: John Wiley, 1990.

———. *Real-Time Strategy.* New York: Harper Business, 1993.

Peter, Laurence J. *The Peter Prescription.* (New Your: 1972: William Morrow & Company Inc.)

Peters, Thomas J. *Thriving on Chaos.* New York: Alfred A. Knopf, 1991.

Peters, Thomas J., and Robert H. Waterman Jr. *In Search of Excellence.* New York: Harper & Row, 1982.

Ritchie, J. B., and Paul Thompson. *Organization and People.* New York: West Publishing, 1976.

Robson, Ross E. *The Quality and Productivity Equation.* Cambridge: Productivity Press, 1990.

Schumacher, E. F. *Small is Beautiful.* New York: Harper & Row, 1975.

Senge, Peter M. *The Fifth Discipline.* New York: Doubleday/Currency, 1990.

Shoenberg, Robert J. *The Art of Being Boss.* New York: New American Library, 1978.

Silk, Leonard, and David Vogel. *Ethics and Profits.* New York: Simon & Schuster, 1976.

Sill, Sterling W. *Leadership, Volume II*. Salt Lake City: Bookcraft, 1960.

Simmons, John & Mares, William. *Working Together*. New York: Alfred A. Knopf, 1983.

Sloma, Richard S. *No-Nonsense Management*. New York: McMillan Publishing, 1977.

Smith, Hyrum W. *The 10 Natural Laws of Successful Time and Life Management*. New York: Warner Books, 1994.

Solman, Paul, and Thomas Friedman. *Life and Death on the Corporate Battlefield*. New York: Simon & Schuster, 1982.

Steers, Richard M., and Lyman W. Porter. *Motivation and Work Behavior*. New York: McGraw-Hill, 1975.

Sudhalter, David L. *The Management Option*. New York: Human Sciences Press, 1980.

The Holy Bible, King James Version.

The Book of Mormon, by permission of The Church of Jesus Christ of Latter-Day Saints. Doubleday, 2004.

The Doctrine & Covenants & The Pearl of Great Price, Salt Lake City, Utah, The Church of Jesus Christ of Latter-Day Saints. 1999.

Tosi, House, and Dunnette Tosi. *Managerial Motivation and Compensation*. Michigan State University, 1972.

Townsend, Robert. *Up the Organization*. New York: Fawcett Crest, 1970.

Vough, Clair F., and Bernard Asbell. *Tapping the Human Resource*. (New York: MACOM, 1975.

Wadia, Maneck S. *Management and the Behavioral Sciences*. Boston: Allyn & Bacon, 1968.

Watson, Thomas J., Jr. *A Business and Its Beliefs.* New York: McGraw-Hill, 1963.

Whiteley, Richard C. *The Customer Driven Company.* New York: Addison-Wesley, 1991.

Work in America Institute Inc., *Productivity through Work Innovations.*

Zuckerman, Marilyn R., and Lewis J. Hatala. *Incredibly American.* Milwaukee: ASQC Quality Press, 1992.

Index

Ronald Reagan 19, 20

S

Sam Walton 17
SAS 70
Sears 84
Semco 70
small farm 22
solar system 4, 40, 223
Southwest Airlines 29
Soviet Union 18, 19
Steve Lohr 10
structure 4, 6, 11, 14, 15, 24, 25,
    38, 39, 40, 41, 62, 63, 192,
    195, 196, 223
superior customer service 22

T

teamwork 4, 11, 15, 84, 204
the dream of freedom 3, 7, 13, 14,
    15, 19, 58, 63, 69, 198, 217,
    219
Total Quality Management 11, 191
Tyco 83

U

US economy 21, 24
US farm industry 23

W

Walter Wriston 63
Waterman 10, 13, 25, 83, 268
Williams Technologies 70
W.L. Gore 43
WorldCom 83
Wrapp 10, 25